BOBBY FLAY'S
BAR AMERICAIN

COOKBOOK

CELEBRATE AMERICA'S GREAT FLAVORS

BOBBY FLAY

WITH STEPHANIE BANYAS
AND SALLY JACKSON

PHOTOGRAPHS BY BEN FINK

CLARKSON POTTER/PUBLISHERS
NEW YORK

Copyright © 2011 by Boy Meets Grill, Inc.
Photographs copyright © 2011 by Ben Fink

All rights reserved.
Published in the United States by Clarkson Potter/Publishers,
an imprint of the Crown Publishing Group, a division of Random House, Inc., New York.
www.crownpublishing.com
www.clarksonpotter.com

CLARKSON POTTER is a trademark and POTTER with colophon
is a registered trademark of Random House, Inc.

Library of Congress Cataloging-in-Publication Data
Flay, Bobby.
  Bobby Flay's Bar Americain cookbook / Bobby Flay, with Stephanie Banyas, and Sally Jackson.
—1st ed.
    p. cm.
  Includes index.
  1. Cookery, American. 2. Bar Americain (New York, N.Y.) I. Banyas, Stephanie. II. Jackson,
Sally, 1978– III. Title. IV. Title: Bar Americain cookbook.
  TX715.F61148 2010
  641.5973—dc22   2009047832

ISBN 978-0-307-46138-4

Printed in China

Design by Wayne Wolf/Blue Cup Creative

10 9 8 7 6 5 4 3 2 1

First Edition

This book is dedicated to my business partner of twenty-plus years, Laurence Kretchmer. Loyal and supportive of my every whim (even the ridiculous ones), he makes the most sincere effort to help me accomplish each one. His dedication to our businesses together is only eclipsed by his unwavering friendship, which I cherish every day.

ACKNOWLEDGMENTS

Peter Hansen
Renee Forsberg
Leia Gaccione
Christopher Foster
Laura Mendez
Alex Roman
Josephine Pacquing
Mark Shay
Liz Jacobson
Angelo Pietrunti
Chrisopher Catanesi
Tyler Pitman
Heidi Vanderwal
Neil Manacle
Vicki Wells
Rick Pitcher
Christine Sanchez
Tara Keeler
Manny Gatdula
Jennifer Lee
Bullfrog & Baum
Jennifer Rudolph Walsh
Jon Rosen
Rockwell Group
Ben Fink
Barb Fritz
Kate Tyler
Jill Browning
Ashley Phillips
Chris Tanigawa
Joan Denman
Doris Cooper
Lauren Shakely
Marysarah Quinn
Dahlia Warner

A special thank-you to:

My assistants and coauthors, Stephanie Banyas and Sally Jackson

My business partners, Laurence Kretchmer, Jerry Kretchmer, and Jeff Bliss

Food Network

The staffs of Mesa Grill New York, Mesa Grill Las Vegas, Mesa Grill Bahamas, Bobby Flay Steak, and Bobby's Burger Palace

And . . .

Rica Allannic, the best editor any author could hope for. Thank you for your steadfast support and your incredible attention to detail.

CONTENTS

INTRODUCTION

Bar Americain is a product of my life's discoveries. I didn't finish high school in a conventional way (I took a test to garner a high school equivalency diploma so that I could apply to culinary school), and as it turns out, I've found I learn best through—well, just living! I am constantly observing, tasting, trying all the world has to offer. Every student, whether a traditional one or not, has a favorite subject, and mine is the foods and culinary traditions of the United States of America. It's been an intense education, one that I hope never ends. And Bar Americain is my translation of that education.

I opened my first restaurant, Mesa Grill, in New York City in 1991 at the age of twenty-five. After running some kitchens for other people earlier on, I had arrived on the scene in a soaring space on lower Fifth Avenue with a bag of chile peppers and a high-profile business partner, Jerry Kretchmer, the owner of Gotham Bar and Grill alongside Chef Alfred Portale. It was exactly what a twenty-five-year-old with seven years of cooking experience and a pocketful of street sense should have—a big, brash, colorful space with big, bold flavors on the plate accompanied by handcrafted margaritas. The place had its own beat—but the rhythm wasn't coming from the speakers, it was coming from the kitchen. Looking back, I wouldn't change a thing. Some twenty years later, Mesa Grill is a New York classic and still running at full speed.

After all the traveling and cooking and eating I've done across the country, the restaurant I was now inspired to open was something different. Both as a native New Yorker and as a student of the city's restaurant business, I know every important restaurant space in town and there was always one in particular that I thought of as my dream space. In fact, my very first meeting with Jerry Kretchmer to discuss the possibility of the two of us teaming up was in that space, a restaurant once called Sam's Cafe. After a brief run, Sam's became JUdson Grill, which Jerry then owned.

JUdson Grill had a good run on West 52nd Street, but it eventually became apparent that something needed to change. Although it was a well-regarded restaurant around town, it was no longer reaching its potential. That's when I called Jerry. I knew this was my chance to grab the space that I had always wanted and I knew just want I wanted to do with it. Bar Americain was born. . . .

The concept and point of view of Bar Americain is simple: it's an American brasserie. As soon as you walk in, you'll sense the echoes of a soaring

European brasserie, with distressed mirrors over the Parisian zinc bar and gorgeous tiles covering the floor. With curved banquettes snaking down the middle of the dining room and a peek into the semi-open kitchen, which is surrounded by a forty-foot-long raw bar, it's a handsome space that radiates brasserie spirit.

I like to tell people that Bar Americain looks brasserie but tastes distinctly American. That raw bar is stocked with the freshest American fish and shellfish, for example. So why the French name? Naming a restaurant can be challenging, and my partners and I had a difficult time coming up with a name that made sense for the space and our vision.

I was in New Mexico doing some chile research for Mesa Grill while the new restaurant was being built. The food media was hassling us for information about the new place, which was soon to open but as of yet nameless and therefore, in the eyes of the press, without a story or a concept. I knew exactly what we were going to serve, but we needed a name to convey that, and fast.

At the time I was reading a book about another chef, a chef who loved spending time in Paris and had one of the most important American restaurants in the country. Jeremiah Tower was at the forefront of New American cuisine when it was born in the early 1980s, when he, Wolfgang Puck, and Alice Waters were leading the way. Jeremiah's San Francisco restaurant, Stars, was a favorite of mine because of how he combined European style with American ingredients and ideas. Yes, we all get inspired somewhere and Stars was the backbone of the inspiration for Bar Americain.

I was reading Jeremiah's book the same day I absolutely needed to name the restaurant, and while reading, I came upon a photo that made me pause. Jeremiah was standing with friends in front of the classic Parisian brasserie La Coupole. Behind them hung the canopy with the name of the restaurant and, in smaller print, the phrase "bar Américain." This was a signal to Americans traveling through Paris earlier in the century that the brasserie served not only wine and beer but also American-style cocktails. While looking at that photograph, it hit me over the head—that's the name! It couldn't be anything else! All the "Stars" aligned right then. I got my partners, Jerry Kretchmer, Laurence Kretchmer, and Jeff Bliss, on a conference call and announced my epiphany, which was at first met with silence, then a question: "Will people think we're just a bar?" No, I was convinced that this had to be the name. Thankfully, my partners agreed.

I often tell people that when I see a map of the United States, I don't see states, cities, and towns—I see ingredients. My eye seeks out those truly American ingredients and the regional dishes that could only be American. And I see people growing and raising our food, cooking their hometown cuisine. I join them as they shout, as loud as they can, that America has arrived. We are a food superpower. Bar Americain celebrates this country's map, delineated by ingredients and culinary culture, as it exists in my mind's eye.

We celebrate with American cocktails, whether an aperitif made with bourbon, like the Kentucky 95, or an appetizer made with lobster and avocado. A bit of Bar Americain's cuisine gets it inspiration from classic French dishes, such as the onion soup, but my take, full of Georgia Vidalia onions and Vermont cheddar cheese, is distinctly homegrown. The choice is yours: whether you select an all-American creamy clam chowder with a sweet potato base; a salad of smoked trout, Kentucky ham, and buttermilk dressing; cornmeal johnny cakes topped with barbecued duck; shrimp and grits; or oyster and lobster shooters, the Bar Americain meal starts with a punch of national pride.

Bar Americain's entrées will fill your table family-style, a way for all to explore my culinary map. Red snapper with a crisp skin of plantains accompanied by avocado, mango, and black beans, which we call Florida-style, celebrates the state's Cuban influence. Or perhaps a rack of pork with a molasses-mustard glaze and a sour mash sauce is more up your alley. And of course, it wouldn't be America without a selection of beef steaks, spice-rubbed and with a host of possible accompanying side dishes, like Brooklyn hash browns and cauliflower goat cheese gratin.

And, trust me, you have to leave room for dessert. . . . Every good brasserie, whether European or American, has a plate of crêpes. Bar Americain's are filled with blueberries and lemon and served with a brown sugar–brown butter sauce. There's a soufflé, of course—mine is laced with blackberries— and a thin apple tart in the style of Paris but with a distinctly American cinnamon sauce as an accompaniment.

I hope this gives you an idea of how I think about Bar Americain. Its concept and its existence are so important to me. Bar Americain is a place of celebration—a place to celebrate good times, good food, good drinks, and the country that made it all possible. It's everything I ever wanted my dream restaurant to be—complete with all the food I love to cook and eat.

COCKTAILS

BLACKBERRY-BOURBON JULEP

Each year on the first Saturday of May, you will find me at Churchill Downs, drink in hand, cheering the horses to victory at the Kentucky Derby. The derby is the first jewel in the Triple Crown of Thoroughbred horseracing and is a magical event steeped in tradition. One of those traditions and the drink in my hand mentioned above is the Mint Julep—bourbon, mint, and sugar served in an ice-frosted silver julep cup. My version of this drink may not be traditional, but it is definitely a winner.

Serves 4

1¼ cups fresh blackberries, plus more for garnish
¼ cup superfine sugar
½ teaspoon vanilla extract
1 cup plus 4 tablespoons bourbon
1 big bunch of fresh mint leaves, plus whole
    sprigs for garnish
Shaved or crushed ice
Club soda, chilled

1. Mash together the blackberries, sugar, and vanilla in a small bowl and let macerate at room temperature until juicy, about 20 minutes. Strain the mixture through a sieve into a bowl, pressing against the solids with a rubber spatula to extract as much juice as possible. Discard the seeds.

2. Put about 2 tablespoons of the blackberry liquid and 1 tablespoon of the bourbon into a silver mint julep cup, add 8 mint leaves, and muddle together.

3. Add shaved ice until the cup is half full. Insert a sprig of mint and then pack in more ice to about 1 inch over the top of the cup. Pour ¼ cup of the bourbon over the ice, add a splash of club soda, and garnish with several big sprigs of mint. Garnish with whole blackberries, if desired.

4. Repeat steps 2 and 3 three times to make 4 drinks. Serve immediately.

PICKLED MARY

The Bloody Mary is probably the most popular brunch cocktail in the United States and with good reason; spiced-up tomato juice and vodka garnished with a stalk of celery—the classic version—is a perfect weekend pick me-up. There are many variations of the Bloody Mary that contain everything from beer to beef bouillon. My version has a southwestern theme, where roasted tomatillo sauce—spiked with vinegar and pickled horseradish—joins tomato juice to give the drink great body while adding a slightly tart, slightly smoky flavor.

Serves 8

6 cups tomato juice

1½ cups Stolichnaya or other good vodka

Tomatillo Sauce (recipe follows)

Juice of 2 lemons

Juice of 3 limes

Few dashes of Worcestershire sauce

Few dashes of Frank's RedHot or other hot sauce

2 tablespoons smoked sweet Spanish paprika

2 teaspoons celery salt

¼ teaspoon cayenne

Celery stalks, for garnish

Whisk together the tomato juice, vodka, tomatillo sauce, lemon and lime juices, Worcestershire sauce, hot sauce, paprika, celery salt, and cayenne in a pitcher. Cover and refrigerate until very cold, at least 2 hours. Serve with celery stalks.

TOMATILLO SAUCE
Makes about 1½ cups

4 large tomatillos, husked and rinsed

½ small red onion, coarsely chopped

2 cloves garlic, chopped

1 jalapeño chile, stemmed and chopped

2 tablespoons canola oil

Kosher salt and freshly ground black pepper

3 tablespoons white wine vinegar

2 tablespoons honey

¼ cup prepared horseradish, drained

6 fresh spinach leaves

¼ cup chopped fresh cilantro

1. Preheat the oven to 400°F.

2. Toss the tomatillos, onion, garlic, and jalapeño with the oil on a baking sheet and season with salt and pepper. Roast in the oven until the mixture is soft but not browned, 15 to 20 minutes. Transfer to a food processor and process until smooth. Add the vinegar, honey, horseradish, spinach, and cilantro and pulse just to combine. Season with salt and pepper. Scrape into a bowl, cover, and refrigerate for at least 2 hours and up to 8 hours before serving.

PICKLED COCKTAIL ONIONS

These onions are a perfect garnish for martinis and Bloody Marys or for eating alongside Country-Style Ribs (page 149) or simply on their own with a cold beer chaser.

Makes 1½ quarts

3 cups apple cider vinegar
½ cup sugar
¼ cup coarsely chopped fresh dill
3 cloves garlic, smashed
1 jalapeño chile, halved
2 tablespoons pickling spice
1½ teaspoons kosher salt
1 pound pearl onions, ends trimmed, peeled

1. Combine the vinegar, 1 cup water, the sugar, dill, garlic, jalapeño, pickling spice, and salt in a medium nonreactive pot and bring to a boil over high heat. Add the onions and cook until a knife inserted into the center meets a little resistance, 4 to 5 minutes.

2. Transfer the mixture to a nonreactive bowl and cover with plastic wrap, or to a large glass jar with a tight-fitting lid, and refrigerate for at least 24 hours before serving. The onions will keep for 1 week in the refrigerator.

PIMM'S CUP

Pimm's No. 1 is a gin-based beverage made from dry gin, liqueur, fruit juices, and spices. When combined with club soda or ginger ale, and a cucumber spear, it becomes a Pimm's Cup. Pimm's No. 1 was created in the mid-eighteenth century by English oyster bar owner James Pimm. The recipe is still a secret; supposedly, only six people know exactly how it is made. It has a dark golden brown color, a medium body, and a taste of quinine, citrus fruits, and spice. Its low alcohol content—only 20 percent—makes it a perfect lunchtime cocktail. The cocktail found its home in the States in New Orleans in the early twentieth century when an anglophile bartender at Napoleon's put it on their menu. The addition of lemonade distinguishes the American version from the classically British Pimm's cup.

Serves 1

3 ounces good-quality lemonade, chilled
2 ounces club soda, chilled
1½ ounces Pimm's No. 1
Cucumber spear, for garnish
Granny Smith apple slice, for garnish

Combine the lemonade, club soda, and Pimm's in a highball glass and garnish with the cucumber and apple.

AMERICAN EAGLE

The cocktail takes its name from the single-barrel ninety-proof bourbon whiskey Eagle Rare, but any high-quality bourbon can be substituted. The small amount of fresh lime juice is needed to add brightness to the drink, not flavor.

Serves 1

Ice cubes
1½ ounces Eagle Rare or other good-quality bourbon
1 ounce Cinnamon Syrup (recipe follows)
2 big dashes of Angostura bitters
1 teaspoon fresh lime juice
1 cinnamon stick

Fill a rocks glass with ice. Add the bourbon, cinnamon syrup, bitters, and lime juice. Garnish with the cinnamon stick.

SIMPLE SYRUP

Simple syrup, or sugar syrup, is very easy to make and is used to sweeten many cocktails as well as iced tea, iced coffee, and even sorbets. The standard ratio is equal parts sugar and water. These recipes can be halved, doubled, or tripled and stored in the refrigerator in a well-sealed container for up to 1 month.

Makes 1 cup (8 ounces)

1 cup sugar
1 cup water

Bring the sugar and water to a boil in a small saucepan over high heat and cook until the sugar is completely melted, a minute or so. Remove from the heat. Transfer to a container with a tight-filling lid and refrigerate until cold, about 1 hour.

VARIATIONS
CINNAMON SYRUP

Bring the sugar, water, and 4 cinnamon sticks to a boil in a small saucepan over high heat and cook until the sugar is completely melted, a minute or so. Remove from the heat. Strain, transfer to a container with a tight-fitting lid, and refrigerate until cold, about 1 hour.

MINT SYRUP

Bring the sugar and water to a boil in a small saucepan over high heat and cook until the sugar is completely melted, a minute or so. Remove from the heat. Add 30 fresh mint leaves and let steep for at least 30 minutes. Strain, transfer to a container with a tight-fitting lid, and refrigerate until cold, about 1 hour.

BARBECUE COCKTAIL

Given my love of grilling and barbecue, this drink was inevitable. Smoky paprika, savory tomato juice, and vodka with a spicy kick meet dry vermouth and tangy lime juice in this cocktail that's perfect with burgers, steaks, fish tacos (page 107), and, well, almost anything barbecued.

Serves 1

Ice cubes

2 ounces jalapeño vodka

¼ ounce dry vermouth

1 ounce tomato juice

½ ounce fresh lime juice, plus ¼ teaspoon for rimming the glass

Pinch of kosher salt, plus ¼ teaspoon for rimming the glass

Pinch of smoked sweet Spanish paprika, plus ¼ teaspoon for rimming the glass

¼ teaspoon sugar, for rimming the glass

Lime twist, for garnish

1. Fill a mixing glass with ice and add the vodka, vermouth, tomato juice, lime juice, salt, and paprika. Stir vigorously until the outside of the glass is beaded with sweat and frosty.

2. Combine the ¼ teaspoon salt, the ¼ teaspoon paprika, and the sugar on a small plate. Wet the rim of a chilled martini glass with the ¼ teaspoon lime juice and dip the rim in the salt mixture. Tap off any excess.

3. Strain the drink into the chilled martini glass and garnish with the lime twist.

B AND TEA

When I am in Kentucky, there are two things that I drink a lot of: sweet tea and bourbon. So, when we were creating our cocktail menu for brunch, it only made sense that I would pair my two favorite southern specialties in one glass.

Serves 1

1½ ounces Jim Beam Black or other good-quality bourbon

1½ ounces strong brewed City Harvest Black or other good-quality black tea, chilled

½ ounce fresh lemon juice

½ ounce fresh lime juice

2 ounces Mint Syrup (page 11)

Orange twist, for garnish

Ice cubes

Fresh mint sprig, for garnish

1. Combine the bourbon, tea, lemon juice, lime juice, and mint syrup in a cocktail shaker and shake for 5 seconds.

2. Rub the orange twist around the inside of a highball glass and then fill the glass with ice. Pour the drink over the ice and garnish with the orange twist and mint sprig.

SANGRITA

Sangrita is actually a spicy cocktail mixer meant to be sipped alternately with shots of tequila. However, it can also make a perfect nonalcoholic option to serve at brunch or as an aperitif. Fresh citrus juice adds a bright note, while the guajillo chile and smoked paprika add earthiness (and, of course, smokiness). Caramelizing the onion instead of adding it raw mellows out the flavor and adds a touch of sweetness.

Serves 8

1 tablespoon canola oil

1 small Spanish onion, halved and thinly sliced

1 guajillo chile, stemmed and seeded

1 (32-ounce) can tomato juice

1 cup fresh orange juice

¼ cup fresh lime juice

1 ounce Simple Syrup (page 11)

1 tablespoon smoked sweet Spanish paprika

1 tablespoon kosher salt

¼ teaspoon freshly ground black pepper

2 dashes of Worcestershire sauce

5 dashes of Tabasco sauce

Lime wedges, for garnish

Silver tequila, for serving (optional)

1. Heat the oil in a medium sauté pan over medium heat. Add the onion and cook, stirring occasionally, until golden brown and caramelized, about 25 minutes. Scrape onto a plate and let cool completely.

2. Meanwhile, put the guajillo chile in a small bowl and cover with boiling water. Let sit for 15 minutes before draining and finely chopping it.

3. Combine the tomato, orange, and lime juices in a pitcher. Stir in the onion, chile, simple syrup, paprika, salt, pepper, Worcestershire sauce, and Tabasco. Cover and refrigerate until cold, at least 2 hours or overnight.

4. Pour into highball glasses and garnish with lime wedges. Serve with shots of tequila if desired.

KENTUCKY 95

Bourbon is a truly American product, with Kentucky producing 95 percent of the world's supply. According to federal law, bourbon must be at least 51 percent corn, distilled to less than 160 proof, and aged for at least two years in new charred-oak barrels. Bourbon also must be made in the United States. In other words, a foreign product that meets all of the other requirements cannot be sold here as bourbon.

I love drinking bourbon straight up or on the rocks and using it in both savory and dessert sauces. It is without a doubt my spirit of choice. I also enjoy mixing it on occasion with other ingredients as long as those ingredients don't mask the slightly woody, slightly floral taste of the bourbon. This drink is an American twist on the French 75, replacing the traditional cognac with bourbon and adding orange juice for freshness.

Serves 1

¾ ounce Maker's Mark or other good-quality bourbon

¾ ounce fresh lemon juice

½ ounce fresh orange juice

¾ ounce Simple Syrup (page 11)

Ice cubes

Champagne or other dry sparkling wine, chilled

Lemon twist, for serving

Combine the bourbon, lemon juice, orange juice, and simple syrup in a cocktail shaker with 6 ice cubes. Shake for 10 seconds before straining into a wineglass and topping with champagne and a lemon twist.

SOUPS AND SALADS

ROASTED CORN SOUP
CRISPY OKRA

This soup delivers a powerful burst of summer. Corn truly is a seasonal ingredient; it's at its best when eaten as soon after it's picked as possible. For most of us, corn season is mid to late summer. Always buy ears of corn that are still in their husks, which should be green and tight around the ears, with silk that is a pale golden green and clings tightly to the kernels. Naturally sweet to begin with, corn intensifies in flavor when roasted. Making a stock with the cobs is a simple, gratifying step for the fullness of corn flavor it delivers. A touch of crème fraîche balances the corn's sweetness and adds a richness to the finished soup while fried rounds of okra provide a nice crunch.

Serves 4

Corn Stock
12 large ears fresh corn, husks and silks removed
1 small Spanish onion, coarsely chopped
1 small stalk celery, coarsely chopped
1 small carrot, coarsely chopped
1 bay leaf

Corn Soup
3 tablespoons olive oil
Kosher salt and freshly ground black pepper
1 tablespoon unsalted butter
6 cloves roasted garlic (see page 250)
¾ cup dry white wine
1 tablespoon sugar, plus more if needed
¼ cup crème fraîche or sour cream
¼ cup Chive Oil (page 239)
Crispy Okra (page 23)

1. Using a sharp knife, slice down each cob to remove the kernels. Scrape the kernels onto a baking sheet and reserve for the soup.

2. Cut each cob in half crosswise and drop them into a large stockpot with the onion, celery, carrot, and bay leaf, and add 2 quarts cold water. Bring to a boil over high heat, reduce the heat to low, and simmer for 30 minutes. Strain the stock into a medium saucepan, bring to a boil, and cook until reduced to about 5 cups. Remove from the heat and let cool slightly.

3. Preheat the oven to 350°F.

4. Add 2 tablespoons of the olive oil to the corn kernels, season with salt and pepper, and toss to coat. Roast the corn in the oven, stirring a few times, until lightly golden brown, about 20 minutes.

5. Heat the remaining tablespoon of oil and the butter in a medium saucepan over medium-high heat. Add the roasted garlic and cook, stirring, for 1 minute. Add the wine, bring to a boil, and cook until almost completely evaporated, a couple of minutes. Add the corn kernels and sugar and cook for 5 minutes, stirring occasionally. Add the corn stock and season with salt and pepper. Bring to a boil, reduce the heat to medium, and let simmer, stirring occasionally, for 30 minutes.

6. Using a slotted spoon, transfer the solids to a blender. Add 2 cups of the cooking liquid and blend until smooth. If the soup is too thick, add more of the cooking liquid, ¼ cup at a time. Strain the soup into a medium saucepan and bring to a simmer over medium heat. Taste for sweetness; if needed, add up to a few extra teaspoons sugar. Whisk in the crème fraîche and season with salt and pepper to taste.

7. Ladle into bowls, drizzle the chive oil over the soup, and top with some of the crispy okra.

SHELLFISH AND ANDOUILLE GUMBO
CRISPY OKRA

Gumbo—it doesn't get much more Louisiana style than that. Louisiana is a prototype for the melting pot of cultures that defines this country; this hearty dish alone can count the cuisines of West Africa, France, and Italy among its influences. Both the Creole and Cajun communities have laid claim to this spicy seafood stew, and I've appropriated a bit from each in this version: the Creole comes in with the tomatoes—that's the Italian presence making itself known—and the Cajun of course is present in the spicy pork andouille sausage. Okra is a traditional gumbo component, and it's usually cooked into the body of the soup. I like the flavor but find that the texture can be a bit slimy. Deep-fried cornmeal-crusted rings of okra solve that problem deliciously.

Serves 6 to 8

½ pound andouille sausage, cut into thin rounds
1 large stalk celery, finely diced
1 large carrot, finely diced
1 large Spanish onion, finely diced
1 red bell pepper, finely diced
3 cloves garlic, finely chopped
8 tablespoons (1 stick) unsalted butter
½ cup all-purpose flour
4 to 5 cups Shrimp Stock (page 241)
1 plum tomato, halved, seeded, and chopped
8 sprigs fresh thyme
2 tablespoons honey
Few dashes of Tabasco sauce
Kosher salt and freshly ground black pepper
4 tablespoons canola oil
12 sea scallops
12 large shrimp, peeled (but tails left on) and deveined
18 oysters, shucked
Crispy Okra (recipe follows)
Chopped fresh cilantro, for garnish
Chopped fresh flat-leaf parsley, for garnish

1. Heat a large sauté pan over high heat. Add the andouille and cook until golden brown on both sides, about 4 minutes. Transfer with a slotted spoon to a plate lined with paper towels.

2. Add the celery, carrot, onion, and bell pepper to the pan and cook in the andouille fat until soft, about 5 minutes. Add the garlic and cook for 1 minute. Remove from the heat.

3. Melt the butter in a large Dutch oven over medium heat. Gradually whisk in the flour. Cook the mixture, whisking occasionally, until it's deep golden brown, 7 to 10 minutes. Scrape the onion mixture into the brown roux and cook for about 3 minutes without stirring.

4. While the roux is cooking, pour the shrimp stock and 1 cup water into a large saucepan and bring to a simmer over low heat.

5. Whisk 4 cups of the stock into the roux. Add the tomato and thyme and bring to a boil, whisking occasionally. Reduce the heat to medium-low, add the andouille sausage, and continue simmering for about 20 minutes, adding more stock or water if the mixture is too thick. Season the mixture with the honey, Tabasco sauce, and salt and pepper to taste. Discard the thyme.

6. Heat 2 tablespoons of the oil in a large sauté pan over high heat until the oil begins to shimmer. Season the scallops with salt and pepper and sear the scallops on one side until golden brown, about 2 minutes. Remove and set aside on a plate.

7. Wipe out the skillet, add the remaining 2 tablespoons oil, and heat over medium-high heat until the oil begins to shimmer. Season the shrimp with salt and pepper and cook until just pink, about 1 minute per side.

8. Add the shrimp, scallops, and oysters to the sauce and continue cooking until the oysters and scallops are just cooked through, about 1 minute.

9. Divide the seafood among large shallow bowls, ladle in some of the broth and sausage, and garnish with the crispy okra and chopped cilantro and parsley.

CRISPY OKRA
Serves 6 to 8 as a garnish

Canola oil, for deep-frying
1½ cups fine yellow cornmeal
Kosher salt and freshly ground black pepper
½ pound okra, sliced ¼ inch thick

1. Heat 2 inches of canola oil in a deep sauté pan over medium heat until it begins to shimmer. Line a baking sheet with paper towels.

2. Pour the cornmeal into a shallow baking dish and season with salt and pepper. Season the okra with salt and pepper and then toss in the cornmeal. Fry the okra in batches, turning once, until golden brown, about 2 minutes. Transfer with a slotted spoon to the paper towels and season with salt. Serve hot.

VIDALIA ONION SOUP
BLISTERED VERMONT CHEDDAR

This soup is a perfect example of one of the things I love to do at Bar Americain: personalize a French brasserie classic with truly American ingredients. This is our American French onion soup. Vidalia onions are a super-sweet variety of onion grown in—and trademarked by!—the state of Georgia. Their sweetness is unmatched, and the slow process of caramelizing them in this recipe intensifies their flavor. (If Vidalia onions aren't unavailable, you can try Walla Wallas from Washington or Hawaii's Maui onions.) Breaking though the browned crust of sharp Vermont cheddar cheese into the molten interior is the first delicious step in devouring this hearty soup. Fresh parsley pesto finishes the dish with a hit of bright color and flavor.

Serves 8

2 tablespoons unsalted butter

2 tablespoons olive oil

3 pounds Vidalia onions, halved and thinly sliced

2 cloves garlic, finely chopped

½ cup brandy

½ cup dry sherry

2 tablespoons all-purpose flour

8 cups chicken stock, homemade (page 240) or store-bought

8 sprigs fresh thyme

Kosher salt and freshly ground black pepper

16 thin slices French baguette, lightly toasted

1 pound aged cheddar cheese, grated

Parsley Pesto (recipe follows)

1. Melt the butter with the oil in a large Dutch oven over medium heat. Add the onions and cook, stirring occasionally, until caramelized, about 40 minutes.

2. Add the garlic and cook for 1 minute. Add the brandy and sherry and boil until almost completely evaporated, about 2 minutes. Stir in the flour and cook for 2 minutes. Whisk in the stock and thyme, bring to a simmer, and cook until the soup is slightly thickened, about 15 minutes. Season with salt and pepper and discard the thyme.

3. Preheat the broiler.

4. Divide eight 16-ounce ovenproof crocks between 2 baking sheets. Put a slice of bread in the bottom of each crock. Fill each crock until three-quarters full. Place another slice of bread in the top of each crock and divide the cheese on top. Carefully slide the crocks under the broiler and broil until the cheese is melted and golden brown, 2 to 3 minutes. Remove from the broiler and top each with a dollop of parsley pesto.

PARSLEY PESTO
Makes about ¾ cup

2 cups packed fresh flat-leaf parsley

1 clove garlic, chopped

3 tablespoons pine nuts

¼ cup extra virgin olive oil

¼ cup freshly grated Parmesan cheese

Kosher salt and freshly ground black pepper

1. Combine the parsley, garlic, and pine nuts in a food processor and process until coarsely chopped. With the motor running, slowly add the oil through the feed tube and process until combined.

2. Add the cheese, season with salt and pepper, and pulse a few times just to incorporate. Scrape into a bowl. The pesto will keep for up to 2 days in a tightly sealed container in the refrigerator. Bring to room temperature before serving.

CHATHAM COD—MANHATTAN CLAM CHOWDER

Chatham is a small town at the "elbow" of Massachusetts' Cape Cod. As it is surrounded by water on three sides, fishing has historically been the major industry of the town. The sweet, mild-flavored cod caught off Chatham's shores is the finest there is. Now, it might seem heretical for a Yankees fan such as I am to give a New England specialty equal billing with a Manhattan clam chowder, but even the Red Sox and the Yankees play on the same team for the All-Star game, right? This all-star dish surrounds creamy roasted potatoes and flaky cod with a tomato-accented broth-based clam chowder. Be sure to use Atlantic razor clams for the garnish. Pacific razor clams are larger and must be cleaned thoroughly and are cooked in a different manner, whereas the smaller Atlantic clam is ready to go!

Serves 4

Chowder Garnish

6 fingerling potatoes, halved lengthwise

4 tablespoons canola oil

Kosher salt and freshly ground black pepper

Juice of 1 lemon

3 tablespoons extra virgin olive oil

2 tablespoons finely chopped fresh flat-leaf
   parsley, plus ¼ cup whole leaves for garnish

½ pound chopped shelled fresh clams
   (littlenecks or cherrystones)

4 (6-ounce) skinless cod fillets

Chowder Broth

1 tablespoon canola oil

½ pound slab bacon, cut crosswise into
   ¼-inch-thick strips

1 small Spanish onion, diced

1 small stalk celery, diced

1 small carrot, diced

3 cloves garlic, chopped

1 cup dry white wine

2 cups bottled clam juice

4 Atlantic razor clams, scrubbed

1 cup pureed canned plum tomatoes

6 black peppercorns

8 sprigs fresh flat-leaf parsley

1. To prepare the chowder garnish, preheat the oven to 400°F.

2. Scatter the potatoes on a baking sheet, toss with 2 tablespoons of the canola oil, and season with salt and pepper. Roast in the oven, turning once, until golden brown and just cooked through, about 15 minutes.

3. Meanwhile, make the chowder broth. Heat the oil in a medium saucepan over medium heat. Add the bacon and cook, stirring occasionally, until golden brown and crispy, about 7 minutes. Transfer the bacon with a slotted spoon to a plate lined with paper towels.

4. Raise the heat under the pan to high, add the onion, celery, and carrot, and cook them in the bacon fat until slightly soft, about 5 minutes. Stir in the garlic and cook for 30 seconds. Add the wine and cook until almost completely evaporated, 2 to 3 minutes; then add the clam juice and bring to a boil. Add the razor clams, cover, and cook until the clams open, about 8 minutes. Transfer the clams to a plate and let cool. Turn the heat down to low under the pan.

5. Once the razor clams are cool enough to handle, shuck and coarsely chop them. For the garnish, whisk together the lemon juice, oil, and chopped parsley in a small bowl. Add the razor clams, season with salt and pepper, and stir to combine. Let the relish sit at room temperature for at least 15 minutes before serving to allow the flavors to meld.

6. Turn the heat up to medium under the pan with the broth. Add the tomato puree, black peppercorns, and parsley sprigs to the broth and bring to a boil. Cook until slightly reduced and thickened, about 5 minutes. Add the chopped littleneck clams and cook for 2 minutes. Discard the parsley.

7. Meanwhile, heat the remaining 2 tablespoons oil in a large nonstick sauté pan over high heat until it just begins to shimmer. Season the fish on both sides with salt and pepper and cook until lightly golden brown on both sides and just cooked through, about 4 minutes per side.

8. Divide the cod among 4 large shallow bowls and ladle the chowder broth over the fish. Arrange the potatoes around the cod and garnish the top of the cod with the razor clam relish, crisp bacon, and whole parsley leaves.

LITTLENECK CLAM AND SWEET POTATO CHOWDER

I have had this chowder on the menu since day one, and no one—neither the patrons nor the staff—will let me take it off. Roasted sweet potato puree thickens the clam broth and imbues it with intense sweet flavor and a vibrant orange hue. That sweetness plays perfectly against the astringent wine and briny clam juice in the broth; a "touch" of rich cream added at the end brings everything lusciously together. Of course, there are also lots of fresh clams, smoky bacon, and (sweet) potato cubes in this hearty soup. Fresh tarragon delivers a touch of delicate anise flavor and a spot of green in the otherwise sunset-orange soup.

Serves 4

Chowder Broth

2 medium sweet potatoes
2 tablespoons unsalted butter
1 medium Spanish onion, coarsely chopped
2 cloves garlic, coarsely chopped
2 tablespoons all-purpose flour
Kosher salt and freshly ground black pepper
½ cup dry white wine
2 to 3 cups bottled clam juice, as needed

Chowder Garnish

1 tablespoon unsalted butter
2 teaspoons canola oil
1 small sweet potato, peeled and cut
    into small dice
Kosher salt and freshly ground black pepper
¼ pound slab applewood-smoked bacon,
    cut into small dice
1 cup dry white wine
16 fresh littleneck or cherrystone clams, scrubbed
2 teaspoons honey
½ cup coarsely chopped shelled fresh clams
    (steamers or cherrystones)
½ cup heavy cream
1 tablespoon finely chopped fresh tarragon

1. To make the chowder broth, preheat the oven to 375°F.

2. Prick the sweet potatoes several times with a fork, place on a baking sheet, and roast in the oven until soft, about 45 minutes. Remove from the oven and let cool slightly. When cool enough to handle, halve each potato lengthwise and, using a small spoon, scrape the flesh into a medium bowl; discard the skins. While the potatoes are still hot, mash with a potato masher or fork until smooth.

3. Heat the butter in a medium saucepan or Dutch oven over medium heat. Add the onion and garlic and cook until soft, about 5 minutes. Stir in the flour and cook for 30 seconds. Stir in the sweet potato puree, season with salt and pepper, and cook until the puree is slightly thickened (you are making a sort of sweet potato roux).

4. Increase the heat to high, add the wine, and cook until completely evaporated, a couple of minutes. Add 2 cups of the clam juice and cook, stirring occasionally, until slightly thickened, 10 to 15 minutes. If the mixture appears to be too thick, thin with a little extra clam juice or water. Season with salt and pepper. Strain the mixture into a bowl and then return the liquid to the saucepan.

5. Meanwhile, prepare the chowder garnish. Melt the butter with the oil in a medium sauté pan over medium heat. Add the diced sweet potato, season with salt and pepper, and cook until golden brown and caramelized, about 10 minutes. Transfer with a slotted spoon to a plate lined with paper towels.

6. Wipe the pan out with paper towels and return it to medium heat. Add the bacon to the hot pan and cook until golden brown and crisp, about 7 minutes. Transfer with a slotted spoon to a plate lined with paper towels.

7. Pour the wine into a medium saucepan and bring to a boil over high heat. Add the clams, cover, and cook until all the clams open, about 4 minutes. Discard any that do not open. Remove the clams with a slotted spoon and place in a bowl.

8. Bring the chowder broth to a simmer over medium heat. Add the sweet potato dice, bacon, and honey and cook for 1 minute. Add the chopped clams and cook for 1 minute. Add the heavy cream and cook until just heated through, about 1 minute.

9. Ladle into bowls and garnish each bowl with a few clams in the shell and a sprinkling of fresh tarragon. Serve immediately.

PUMPKIN SOUP
CRANBERRY-MAPLE CRÈME FRAÎCHE, TOASTED PUMPKIN SEEDS, CHIVES

All of the best flavors of an American Thanksgiving are featured in this fall soup. The benefit of using vegetable stock is twofold: most important to me is taste— vegetable stock, as opposed to rich chicken stock, melds seamlessly with the pumpkin, thinning its body without competing with the flavor. It also means that this soup is a perfect option for vegetarian guests. Trust me; everyone at the table with be happy with this tasty offering.

Serves 8

  2 (15-ounce) cans pumpkin puree, *not* flavored
      pie filling (about 3½ cups)
  3 to 4½ cups vegetable stock or chicken stock,
      homemade (page 241 or 240) or
      store-bought, as needed
  1 teaspoon ground cinnamon
  ½ teaspoon ground Mexican cinnamon (canela)
      or additional ground cinnamon
  ½ teaspoon ground allspice
  ½ teaspoon ground cloves
  3 tablespoons honey
  1 tablespoon pure maple syrup
  ¼ cup crème fraîche or sour cream
  Kosher salt and freshly ground black pepper

  Cranberry-Maple Crème Fraîche (recipe follows)
  ⅓ cup pumpkin seeds, toasted (see page 250)
  ¼ cup finely chopped fresh chives

1. Put the pumpkin puree in a large saucepan, whisk in 3 cups of the stock, and bring to a simmer over medium heat. Add the cinnamon, Mexican cinnamon, allspice, cloves, honey, and maple syrup. Simmer for 15 to 20 minutes.

2. Whisk in up to 1½ cups more stock if the soup is too thick. Remove from the heat and whisk in the crème fraîche. Season with salt and pepper to taste.

3. Ladle the soup into bowls and top each with a large dollop of the cranberry-maple crème fraîche and some of the pumpkin seeds and chives.

CRANBERRY-MAPLE CRÈME FRAÎCHE
Makes about 1¼ cups

  2 cups cranberry juice
  2 tablespoons pure maple syrup
  ¼ teaspoon maple extract
  1 cup crème fraîche or sour cream
  Kosher salt

1. Bring the cranberry juice to a boil in a small saucepan over high heat. Cook, stirring occasionally, until thickened and reduced to ¼ cup, about 10 minutes. Remove from the heat, stir in the maple syrup and maple extract, and let cool to room temperature.

2. Put the crème fraîche into a small bowl, add the cranberry mixture, and stir to combine. Season with salt. Cover and refrigerate for at least 30 minutes and up to 1 day to allow the flavors to meld.

BOSTON LETTUCE SALAD
BACON, POACHED EGG, BUTTERMILK-BLUE CHEESE DRESSING

Once you taste this dressing, you'll be reluctant to use a bottled variety again. Given how extremely simple—and quick—it is to prepare, you won't need to. Crisped cubes of bacon, eggs, and blue cheese often come together over a bed of bitter frisée, but I think that tender Boston lettuce makes a superb substitution. Its sweet leaves get some punch from peppery radishes and the tangy buttermilk-based dressing.

Serves 4

¼ pound thick-cut bacon, cut crosswise into ¼-inch strips
1 tablespoon white wine vinegar
4 large eggs
Kosher salt and freshly ground black pepper
Buttermilk–Blue Cheese Dressing (recipe follows)
1 head of Boston lettuce, leaves separated
White Wine Vinaigrette (recipe follows)
3 radishes, thinly sliced
2 ounces Maytag blue cheese, crumbled
2 tablespoons finely chopped fresh chives

1. Cook the bacon in a medium sauté pan over medium heat, stirring occasionally, until golden brown and the fat has rendered, about 10 minutes. Transfer with a slotted spoon to a plate lined with paper towels.

2. Bring 1 quart cold water and the vinegar to a simmer in a deep sauté pan. Break the eggs, one at a time, into a ramekin and carefully slide each egg into the simmering water. Simmer until the whites are firm but the yolks are still runny, about 3 minutes. Transfer with a slotted spoon to a plate lined with paper towels and season with salt and pepper to taste.

3. Put a large dollop of the buttermilk–blue cheese dressing in the center of each of 4 large dinner plates.

4. Place the lettuce leaves in a large bowl, toss with half of the white wine vinaigrette, and season with salt and pepper. Arrange the leaves on top of the buttermilk-blue cheese dressing.

5. Divide the eggs, bacon, and radishes among the plates and drizzle with more of the white wine vinaigrette. Garnish with the blue cheese and chives.

BUTTERMILK–BLUE CHEESE DRESSING
Makes about ½ cup

¼ cup buttermilk
¼ cup sour cream
1 tablespoon fresh lemon juice
2 ounces Maytag blue cheese, crumbled (½ cup)
Kosher salt and freshly ground black pepper

Put the buttermilk, sour cream, and lemon juice in a blender and blend until combined. With the motor running, slowly add the blue cheese and blend until smooth. Season with salt and pepper. The dressing can be made 1 day in advance and stored in a container with a tight-fitting lid in the refrigerator.

WHITE WINE VINAIGRETTE
Makes about ½ cup

3 tablespoons white wine vinegar
1½ teaspoons Dijon mustard
1 teaspoon honey
Kosher salt and freshly ground black pepper
⅓ cup canola oil

Whisk together the vinegar, mustard, and honey in a small bowl. Season with salt and pepper. Slowly whisk in the oil until emulsified. The dressing can be made 1 day in advance and stored in a container with a tight-fitting lid in the refrigerator.

CHOPPED APPLE SALAD
TOASTED WALNUTS, BLUE CHEESE, POMEGRANATE VINAIGRETTE

This is a sophisticated take on an American classic, the Waldorf salad. Tart crisp apples, piquant blue cheese, and rich, crunchy walnuts combine to create a salad with layers of flavor and texture. Slightly sweet, deliciously tangy pomegranate molasses is the key ingredient in the vinaigrette, binding all of the elements in place of the traditional mayonnaise-based dressing. Tender baby spinach and crisp endive amp up the fresh factor of this hearty salad.

Serves 6 to 8

4 apples such as Granny Smith, Gala, or Fuji, cored and cut into ½-inch dice

2 ounces baby spinach

2 large heads of Belgian endive, thinly sliced crosswise

1½ cups coarsely chopped walnuts, toasted (see page 250)

½ pound blue cheese such as Maytag, crumbled (2 cups)

Pomegranate Vinaigrette (recipe follows)

Kosher salt and freshly ground black pepper

Combine the apples, spinach, endive, walnuts, and blue cheese in a large bowl. Add the vinaigrette and toss to coat. Season with salt and pepper to taste.

POMEGRANATE VINAIGRETTE
Makes about 1 cup

3 tablespoons pomegranate molasses

2 tablespoons red wine vinegar

1 heaping tablespoon Dijon mustard

1 tablespoon honey, or more to taste

Kosher salt and freshly ground black pepper

⅔ cup extra virgin olive oil

Whisk together the pomegranate molasses, vinegar, mustard, and honey in a medium bowl. Season with salt and pepper. Slowly whisk in the olive oil until emulsified. The dressing can be made 2 days in advance and stored in a container with a tight-fitting lid in the refrigerator.

FRIED GREEN TOMATO SALAD
SMOKED TROUT, FAVA BEANS, ROASTED BEETS, SWEET AND SOUR DRESSING

This fresh and satisfying salad gets its inspiration from two very different locales: the sweet and sour dressing is indebted to the Pennsylvania Dutch, while the fried green tomatoes come straight from the South. The brightly hued dressing is just the thing to enhance the interplay of tart green tomatoes; sweet, earthy beets; buttery fava beans; and tangy, creamy goat cheese. Green tomatoes and fava beans are two crops that I particularly look forward to seeing at the first farmers' markets of spring, and this salad is a delicious way to celebrate the best of that season. If you can't find fava beans, lima beans are a fair substitute.

Serves 4

1 red beet, trimmed and scrubbed
1 yellow beet, trimmed and scrubbed
1 cup plus 2 tablespoons canola oil
Kosher salt and freshly ground black pepper
1/2 pound shelled fresh or frozen fava beans
8 (1/2-inch-thick) slices green tomatoes
     (about 3 green tomatoes)
2 cups coarse yellow cornmeal
Sweet and Sour Dressing (recipe follows)
3/4 pound smoked rainbow trout fillet, cut into
     8 pieces
2 tablespoons trout roe (optional)
1/2 cup microgreens, for garnish

1. Preheat the oven to 375°F.

2. Place each beet in the center of a large piece of heavy-duty aluminum foil, drizzle with 2 tablespoons of the oil, and season with salt and pepper. Wrap the beets tightly, place on a baking sheet, and roast in the oven until tender, about 1 hour. Remove the beets from the oven, let cool slightly, and then remove the skins. Cut each beet into 1/2-inch dice.

3. Bring 3 cups water to a boil in a medium saucepan and add 1 tablespoon salt. Add the fava beans and cook until just tender, about 2 minutes. Drain in a colander, rinse with cold water, and drain again. If using fresh favas, remove their outer layer.

4. Place the sliced tomatoes on a baking sheet lined with paper towels to remove some of the excess moisture. Season both sides with salt and pepper. Put the cornmeal in a large shallow bowl and season with salt and pepper. Dredge the tomatoes in the cornmeal on both sides and tap off the excess cornmeal.

5. Heat the 1 cup of oil in a large sauté pan over medium-high heat until it begins to shimmer. Four at a time, fry the tomatoes until golden brown on both sides and just cooked through, about 1 1/2 minutes per side. Transfer with a slotted spatula to the baking sheet lined with fresh paper towels and season with salt.

6. Drizzle some of the sweet and sour dressing on the bottom of 4 dinner plates. Place 2 fried green tomatoes on each plate. Scatter the beets and fava beans around the tomatoes and top each tomato with some of the smoked trout. Scoop 1 1/2 teaspoons of the trout roe on top of each portion of fish if desired. Garnish with the microgreens.

SWEET AND SOUR DRESSING
Makes about ¾ cup

½ cup plus 1 tablespoon canola oil
2 cloves garlic, finely chopped
3 tablespoons red wine vinegar
1 tablespoon fresh lemon juice
1 tablespoon ketchup
1 tablespoon tomato paste
2 teaspoons Dijon mustard
2 teaspoons honey
Kosher salt and freshly ground black pepper
1 large green onion, green and pale green parts,
    thinly sliced

1. Heat 1 tablespoon of the oil in a small sauté pan over medium-low heat. Add the garlic and cook, stirring occasionally, until it turns light golden brown, about 1½ minutes. Remove from the heat and let cool slightly.

2. Whisk together the garlic, vinegar, lemon juice, ketchup, tomato paste, mustard, and honey in a medium bowl. Season with salt and pepper. Slowly whisk in the remaining ½ cup oil until emulsified and then stir in the green onion. The dressing can be made 1 day in advance and stored in a tightly covered container in the refrigerator. Bring to room temperature before using.

WILD MUSHROOM SALAD
QUINOA, AGED GOAT CHEESE, CARAMELIZED SHALLOT MARMALADE

Quinoa is a so-called ancient grain recently rediscovered by the modern cook. With a toothsome texture and nutty, earthy flavor, quinoa is also loaded with fiber, omega-3 fatty acids, and vitamin B—even iron! I'm happy to say that it is as delicious as it is healthy. Wild mushrooms reinforce the earthiness of the grain, and aged goat cheese (I like one from New York Hudson Valley's Coach Farm) brings a sharp focus to the salad. Though more savory than not, the caramelized shallots provide a sweet note to balance the salad's other components. This comforting salad is a perfect late-fall dish.

Serves 4

½ pound cremini mushrooms, stemmed and thinly sliced

½ pound oyster mushrooms, coarsely chopped

3 shiitake mushrooms, stemmed, halved, and thinly sliced crosswise

½ cup plus 2 tablespoons extra virgin olive oil

Kosher salt and freshly ground black pepper

¼ cup aged balsamic vinegar

2 teaspoons finely chopped fresh thyme

¼ cup finely chopped fresh flat-leaf parsley, plus whole leaves for garnish

1 cup quinoa

4 ounces mesclun greens

2 teaspoons white truffle oil (optional)

Caramelized Shallots (recipe follows)

12 (¼-inch-thick) slices French baguette, toasted

1 (6-ounce) log aged goat cheese, such as Coach Farm, cut into 12 slices

1. Preheat the oven to 400°F.

2. Put the mushrooms in a roasting pan or on a rimmed baking sheet, toss with 2 tablespoons of the oil, and season with salt and pepper. Roast in the oven, stirring a few times, until soft and golden brown, about 25 minutes.

3. Meanwhile, whisk together the remaining ½ cup oil, the vinegar, thyme, and chopped parsley and season with salt and pepper. Reserve 3 tablespoons of the vinaigrette in a small bowl.

4. Add the warm mushrooms to the remaining vinaigrette, season with salt and pepper, and stir to combine. Let the mixture sit at room temperature for at least 30 minutes to marinate.

5. Put the quinoa grains into a fine-mesh strainer and rinse under cold running water for 1 minute. Drain well. Transfer the quinoa to a medium saucepan. Add 2 cups cold water and 1 tablespoon salt, cover the pot, and bring to a boil over high heat. Reduce the heat to low and cook until the quinoa is tender and the water has evaporated, about 18 minutes. Turn off the heat and let stand for 10 minutes without lifting the cover. Spoon the quinoa into the marinated mushrooms and stir to combine.

6. Put the greens in a large bowl, toss with the reserved balsamic vinaigrette, and season with salt and pepper. Divide the greens among 4 large plates and top the greens with some of the quinoa-mushroom salad. Drizzle the quinoa salad with the truffle oil, if using, season with additional pepper, and garnish with parsley leaves.

7. Spread some of the caramelized shallots over the toasted bread and top with a slice of cheese. Place 3 croutons around the perimeter of each plate.

CARAMELIZED SHALLOTS
Makes enough for 12 slices baguette

1 tablespoon unsalted butter
1 tablespoon olive oil
8 large shallots, thinly sliced
2 tablespoons light muscovado sugar
½ cup red wine vinegar
2 teaspoons finely chopped fresh thyme
Kosher salt and freshly ground black pepper

1. Melt the butter with the oil in a medium sauté pan over medium heat. Add the shallots and cook, stirring occasionally, until softened and golden brown, 20 to 25 minutes.

2. Add the sugar and vinegar and cook until the mixture thickens and becomes jamlike, about 15 minutes. If the mixture becomes too thick to spread, stir in a tablespoon or so of water.

3. Add the thyme and season with salt and pepper. Remove and let cool to room temperature. The marmalade will keep for 2 days in a tightly sealed container in the refrigerator. Bring to room temperature before serving.

CALIFORNIA-STYLE BLUE CRAB SALAD
AVOCADO, NIÇOISE OLIVES, MEYER LEMON DRESSING

This salad is a refreshing choice for an elegant lunch on a summer day. Succulent crab, creamy cubes of avocado, salty olives, and sweet grape tomatoes are folded into a mixture of cool mayonnaise and bright red wine vinegar. Cayenne pepper and Spanish paprika add a touch of heat and depth to the mix. Mesclun greens tossed in a sunny Meyer lemon dressing make the crab salad's bed.

Sweet blue crabs are found in the waters of the Atlantic and the Gulf of Mexico. Their silky texture and rich taste make them my crab of choice—no matter from where a dish's inspiration may come.

Serves 4

3/4 cup mayonnaise

2 tablespoons red wine vinegar

2 tablespoons smoked sweet Spanish paprika

1/8 teaspoon cayenne

Kosher salt and freshly ground black pepper

1 1/2 pounds jumbo lump blue crab meat, picked over

1 ripe Hass avocado, halved, pitted, peeled, and thinly sliced

1/2 cup pitted and coarsely chopped Niçoise olives

1 cup grape tomatoes, halved

1/4 cup finely chopped fresh chives

1 ounce microgreens

1/2 recipe Meyer Lemon Dressing (page 45)

1. Whisk together the mayonnaise, vinegar, paprika, and cayenne in a large bowl. Season with salt and pepper. Add the crab, avocado, olives, tomatoes, and chives and fold gently to combine.

2. Put the greens in a large bowl, toss with the Meyer lemon dressing, and season with salt and pepper. Arrange the greens on 4 large dinner plates and top each with a mound of the crab salad.

KENTUCKY HAM
BLACK MISSION FIGS, PECANS, RICOTTA, MOLASSES-MUSTARD DRESSING

This salad is a showcase for fresh figs. They make a brief appearance in most marketplaces, so you've got to make the most of their honey-sweet flesh when you can. Slices of richly flavored, smoky-salty Kentucky ham make a fantastic pairing. Kentucky ham is a dry-cured country ham comparable to an Italian prosciutto or Spanish Serrano ham. While you could substitute either, I love both the taste and the homegrown appeal of Kentucky ham. Sweet pecans add a bit of crunch to the salad, and the tangy molasses-mustard vinaigrette enhances its southern vibe.

Serves 4

¼ pound baby arugula
5 fresh figs, preferably Black Mission, quartered
Molasses-Mustard Dressing (recipe follows)
Kosher salt and freshly ground black pepper
¼ pound thinly sliced country ham
½ cup pecans, toasted (see page 250)
2 green onions, green and pale green parts,
　　thinly sliced
4 (½-inch-thick) slices country bread, grilled
　　until marked
½ cup ricotta cheese

1. Put the arugula and figs in a large bowl. Add half of the dressing, season with salt and pepper, and toss gently to coat the ingredients.

2. Divide the greens and figs among 4 large plates. Place a slice or two of ham on the side of each, drizzle with more of the dressing, and garnish with the pecans and green onions. Top the grilled bread with the ricotta and serve alongside the salad.

MOLASSES-MUSTARD DRESSING
Makes about ¾ cup

3 tablespoons molasses
1½ tablespoons red wine vinegar
1½ tablespoons Dijon mustard
1 teaspoon honey
½ teaspoon kosher salt
¼ teaspoon freshly ground black pepper
½ cup canola oil

Combine the molasses, 2 tablespoons water, the vinegar, mustard, honey, salt, and pepper in a medium bowl and whisk until combined. Slowly whisk in the oil until emulsified. The dressing can be made 1 day in advance and stored in a tightly covered container in the refrigerator.

WARM LENTIL SALAD
ROASTED BEETS, GOAT CHEESE

Tangy goat cheese and sweet beets are a famously good pairing; it is with good reason that so many French brasseries and bistros have a salad featuring the two on their menus. Lentils are another ingredient favored in France, and the combination of the three makes for one very satisfying salad. (Crispy bits of smoky bacon don't hurt either.) I don't recommend cheating with canned lentils. The texture and flavor of dried lentils cooked in a well-seasoned stock is far superior, and they cook up in no time.

Serves 4

3 medium red or gold beets, trimmed
   and scrubbed
3 tablespoons canola oil
2 small carrots, 1 quartered and 1 finely diced
1 medium Spanish onion, quartered
1 small stalk celery, quartered
1 bay leaf
5 sprigs fresh thyme, plus 2 teaspoons
   finely chopped
1 quart chicken stock, homemade (page 240)
   or store-bought
1¼ cups dried French green lentils
Kosher salt and freshly ground black pepper
¼ pound slab bacon, diced
2 cloves garlic, finely chopped
2 tablespoons sherry vinegar
3 ounces chopped frisée or mixed greens
Sherry Vinaigrette (recipe follows)
4 (½-inch-thick) slices fresh goat cheese

1. Preheat the oven to 375°F.

2. Put each beet on its own piece of aluminum foil. Drizzle with 2 tablespoons of the oil. Wrap the beets tightly, place on a baking sheet, and roast in the oven until cooked through, about 1 hour. Remove the beets from the oven, let cool slightly, and then remove the skins. Cut into ¼-inch-thick slices.

3. Place the quartered carrot, onion, and celery and the bay leaf, thyme sprigs, and chicken stock in a medium saucepan. Bring to a boil, stir in the lentils, and season with salt and pepper. Reduce the heat to medium-low and cook until the lentils are tender, about 25 minutes. Drain well and discard the carrot, onion, celery, bay leaf, and thyme.

4. Heat the remaining 1 tablespoon oil in a large sauté pan over medium heat, add the bacon, and cook until crisp and golden brown, about 8 minutes. Transfer the bacon with a slotted spoon to a dish lined with paper towels. Add the garlic and diced carrot to the pan and cook until soft, about 5 minutes. Add the cooked lentils and bacon and stir to combine. Stir in the chopped thyme and sherry vinegar and season with salt and pepper to taste. Keep warm.

5. Place the frisée in a large bowl, toss with half of the vinaigrette, and season with salt and pepper. Arrange the roasted beets around the outside of 4 dinner plates and the frisée in the centers. Top the frisée with the warm lentils and place a slice of goat cheese on top of each. Drizzle the salads with the remaining vinaigrette.

SHERRY VINAIGRETTE
Makes ¾ cup

¼ cup sherry vinegar
1 tablespoon Dijon mustard
2 teaspoons honey
¼ teaspoon kosher salt
¼ teaspoon freshly ground black pepper
½ cup extra virgin olive oil

Whisk together the vinegar, mustard, and honey in a small bowl. Season with the salt and pepper. Slowly whisk in the oil until emulsified. The dressing can be made 1 day in advance and stored in a tightly covered container in the refrigerator. Bring to room temperature before using.

ASPARAGUS CHOPPED SALAD
VERMONT CHEDDAR, MEYER LEMON DRESSING

The joy of a chopped salad is that there is no need to compose each forkful to make sure you have the perfect bite—every uniformly sized morsel is already tossed and mixed together for a whole plate full of perfect bites. Green, almost grassy in flavor, asparagus is one of spring's delights. Grilling enhances its flavor and imparts a pleasant bit of char to the salad. Briny olives, sharp cheddar cheese, and tender chickpeas add substance to the mix, while crispy bits of fried pita bread lend a salty crunch and additional texture. (We make our own pita chips at the restaurant, and the directions to do so are here, but you could certainly skip this step and use crumbles of your favorite bagged pita chips instead.) Slightly sweet, slightly tart, definitely delicious, this Meyer lemon dressing pops with whole grain mustard, lemon zest, and honey.

Serves 4 to 6

- 2 cups plus 2 tablespoons canola oil
- 2 pocketless pitas, halved and sliced ¼ inch thick
- Kosher salt and freshly ground black pepper
- 16 medium spears asparagus, trimmed
- 6 ounces mesclun greens
- 1 cup grape tomatoes, halved
- ½ pound aged white cheddar cheese, cut into ½-inch dice
- 1 English cucumber, cut into ½-inch dice
- ½ cup pitted and coarsely chopped kalamata olives
- 1 cup drained canned chickpeas, rinsed and drained again
- Meyer Lemon Dressing (recipe follows)

1. Heat 2 cups of the canola oil in a medium saucepan over medium heat until it reaches 360°F on a deep fat thermometer. Fry the pita slices, in batches, until lightly golden brown and crisp, turning once, about 1 minute. Transfer with a slotted spoon to a plate lined with paper towels and season with salt and pepper.

2. Preheat a grill to high or heat a grill pan over high heat. Brush the asparagus with the remaining 2 tablespoons oil and season with salt and pepper. Grill the asparagus, turning once, until crisp-tender, 4 to 6 minutes. Transfer to a cutting board and cut on the bias into 1-inch-long pieces.

3. Combine the mesclun, tomatoes, cheese, cucumber, olives, chickpeas, and asparagus in a large bowl. Add half of the dressing, season with salt and pepper, and toss well to coat. Divide the salad among large dinner plates. Drizzle with more of the dressing and top with the pita chips.

MEYER LEMON DRESSING
Makes about ¾ cup

- ½ teaspoon finely grated lemon zest
- ¼ cup fresh Meyer lemon juice, or 3 tablespoons fresh lemon juice plus 1 tablespoon fresh orange juice
- 1 tablespoon red wine vinegar
- 2 tablespoons mayonnaise
- 1 heaping tablespoon whole grain mustard
- 2 teaspoons honey
- Kosher salt and freshly ground black pepper
- ½ cup extra virgin olive oil

Whisk together the lemon zest and juice, vinegar, mayonnaise, mustard, and honey in a medium bowl. Season with salt and pepper. Slowly whisk in the oil until emulsified. The dressing can be made 1 day in advance and stored in a container with a tight-fitting lid in the refrigerator.

SANDWICHES

GRILLED CHEESE ♦ AGED CHEDDAR, GOAT CHEESE, BACON, GREEN TOMATO   49

LOBSTER CLUB ♦ GREEN ONION DRESSING, CRISPY HAM, ARUGULA   50

KENTUCKY HOT BROWN   52

GRILLED SWORDFISH CLUB ♦ AVOCADO, LEMON MAYONNAISE   54

PULLED BARBECUED DUCK SANDWICH ♦ COLESLAW, SPICY PICKLES   56

CEDAR-PLANKED BURGER ♦ RED WINE BARBECUE SAUCE, CHEDDAR CHEESE, SAUTÉED MUSHROOMS   60

GREEN CHILE CHEESEBURGER   62

BISON REUBEN SANDWICH ♦ HUNDRED ISLAND DRESSING   64

GRILLED CHEESE
AGED CHEDDAR, GOAT CHEESE, BACON, GREEN TOMATO

This is the ultimate grilled cheese. Forget about American cheese; this grown-up grilled cheese features the real deals. I love goat cheese, but you couldn't do this sandwich without the cheddar; goat cheese can be too crumbly to melt well, and cheddar—beyond having great flavor—gets all nice and gooey when melted, bringing all of the tasty components together. Tart green tomatoes balance the salty bacon, which is a big part of what makes this sandwich so amazing. One final note: A key factor in making any grilled cheese is to be sure the bread is well toasted.

Serves 4

8 (¼-inch-thick) slices double-smoked bacon

8 tablespoons (1 stick) unsalted butter, softened

8 (1-inch-thick) slices Pullman or other
   good-quality white sandwich bread

8 (½-inch-thick) slices sharp cheddar cheese

6 ounces fresh goat cheese, cut into 8 slices

2 green tomatoes, each cut into 4 slices

Kosher salt and freshly ground black pepper

1 ounce baby arugula

Whole grain Dijon mustard (optional)

1. Place the bacon in a large cast-iron griddle or sauté pan over medium heat and cook until golden brown and crisp, about 4 minutes per side. Transfer to a plate lined with paper towels. Clean the griddle and return to medium heat.

2. Spread the butter on one side of each slice of bread. Place 4 of the slices, buttered side down, on a cutting board or other clean flat surface. Top each slice of bread with 2 slices cheddar, 2 slices goat cheese, 2 slices tomato, and 2 slices bacon and season with salt and pepper. Place the remaining bread slices on top, buttered side up.

3. Cook the sandwiches on the griddle until golden brown on both sides and the cheddar cheese has melted, about 3 minutes per side. Remove from the griddle. Open each sandwich and stuff some arugula into each one. Serve the sandwiches with mustard on the side, if desired, for dipping.

LOBSTER CLUB
GREEN ONION DRESSING, CRISPY HAM, ARUGULA

The standard club sandwich layers turkey or chicken with bacon. Dressed up with lobster salad and thin slices of country ham, this sandwich is anything but standard. The fresh green onion dressing, both a component of the lobster salad and spread on the bread, has real impact in flavor and in presentation. The sandwich is amazing served on buttery, slightly spicy Chipotle Brioche, but a good-quality white Pullman loaf will certainly do in a pinch. Serve with a side of Barbecued Potato Chips (page 163) to complete the Bar Americain experience.

Serves 4

½ cup canola oil
4 thin slices country ham
¾ cup mayonnaise
2 tablespoons fresh lemon juice
1 heaping tablespoon Dijon mustard
1 heaping tablespoon whole grain mustard
1 small stalk celery, thinly sliced
2 green onions, green and pale green parts, thinly sliced
¼ cup finely diced red onion
¼ cup finely chopped fresh flat-leaf parsley
Kosher salt and freshly ground black pepper
1½ pounds cooked fresh lobster meat, chopped
8 (½-inch-thick) slices Chipotle Brioche (page 194), lightly toasted
Green Onion Dressing (recipe follows)
1 ounce arugula leaves

1. Heat the oil in a large sauté pan over high heat until the oil begins to shimmer. Working in batches, carefully add 2 slices of the ham at a time and cook until crispy on both sides, about 2 minutes. Transfer to a plate lined with paper towels.

2. Whisk together the mayonnaise, lemon juice, both mustards, the celery, green onions, red onion, and parsley in a medium bowl and season with salt and pepper. Fold in the lobster meat.

3. Spread each slice of bread with some of the green onion dressing. Divide half of the arugula among 4 slices of the bread. Top the arugula with some of the lobster salad and a slice of crisp ham. Place the remaining arugula on top of the ham and top with the remaining bread.

GREEN ONION DRESSING
Makes about ¾ cup

¼ cup mayonnaise
3 tablespoons white wine vinegar
2 teaspoons honey
¼ cup canola oil
Kosher salt and freshly ground black pepper
5 green onions, green and pale green parts, chopped

Combine the mayonnaise, vinegar, honey, and oil in a blender and blend until combined. Season with salt and pepper. Add the green onions and pulse a few times just to incorporate. You do not want to puree it; there should be specks of green in the dressing. Scrape into a bowl. The dressing is best made the same day it will be used.

KENTUCKY HOT BROWN

The Kentucky sandwich. Built on a base of savory French toast, this open-faced sandwich needs no doubling up. Thick slices of turkey breast and juicy tomatoes are topped with a decadent cheese sauce, broiled until bubbly and golden brown, then crowned with crisp slices of bacon. It's no surprise that this dish, named for its birthplace at the Brown Hotel in Louisville, has become Kentucky Derby lore.

Serves 4 or 8

Roast Turkey and Sauce

1 boneless turkey breast, about 3 pounds

6 tablespoons (¾ stick) unsalted butter, softened

Kosher salt and freshly ground black pepper

2 cups whole milk, plus more if needed

2 tablespoons all-purpose flour

½ pound sharp white cheddar cheese, grated (2 cups)

¼ cup freshly grated Parmesan cheese

Pinch of freshly grated nutmeg

Sandwiches

4 large eggs

1½ cups whole milk, or more if needed

Kosher salt and freshly ground black pepper

8 (½-inch-thick) slices day-old Pullman or other good-quality white sandwich bread

4 tablespoons (½ stick) unsalted butter

6 tablespoons canola oil

3 ripe beefsteak tomatoes, sliced ½ inch thick

6 ounces sharp white cheddar cheese, grated (1½ cups)

½ cup freshly grated Parmesan cheese

16 (¼-inch-thick) slices bacon, cooked until crisp (see page 49)

Fresh flat-leaf parsley leaves, for garnish

1. To roast the turkey, preheat the oven to 425°F.

2. Rub the entire breast with 4 tablespoons butter and season with salt and pepper. Place in a small roasting pan and roast for 15 minutes. Reduce the heat to 350°F and continue roasting the turkey until a thermometer inserted into the center registers 155°F, 1 to 1½ hours. Remove from the oven, tent loosely with foil, and let rest for 10 minutes before slicing.

3. To make the sauce, put the milk in a small saucepan and bring to a simmer over low heat. Melt the remaining 2 tablespoons butter over medium-high heat in a medium saucepan. Whisk in the flour and cook for 1 minute. Gradually whisk in the hot milk.

Bring to a boil and cook, whisking constantly, until thickened and the raw flour taste has cooked out, 4 to 5 minutes. Stir in more milk if the sauce is too thick to pour.

4. Remove from the heat and whisk in the cheddar and Parmesan cheeses, whisking until the cheddar has melted. Season with the nutmeg and salt and pepper to taste. Keep warm.

5. To make the sandwiches, whisk together the eggs and milk in a medium baking dish. Season with salt and pepper. Dip each slice of bread in the mixture and let sit until completely soaked through, about 10 seconds per side.

6. Heat 1 tablespoon of the butter and 1 tablespoon of the oil in a large nonstick sauté pan over medium-high heat. Working in batches, cook 2 slices of the bread at a time until golden brown on both sides, about 2 minutes per side. Repeat with the remaining butter, 3 tablespoons oil, and bread.

7. Preheat the broiler.

8. Put the tomatoes on a rimmed baking sheet, brush with the remaining 2 tablespoons oil, and season with salt and pepper. Broil until slightly charred and just cooked through, 3 to 4 minutes.

9. Place 4 slices of the egg bread on a baking sheet, slide under the broiler, and heat just to warm through, 20 seconds on each side. Repeat with the remaining bread.

10. Top each slice of bread with 2 to 3 slices turkey. Ladle sauce over the top and divide the cheddar and Parmesan over the top of each slice. Place under the broiler and cook until bubbly and the tops are golden brown, about 2 minutes. Remove from the oven, top each slice with 2 slices of bacon and a tomato slice, and sprinkle with parsley.

GRILLED SWORDFISH CLUB
AVOCADO, LEMON MAYONNAISE

This was on Bar Americain's lunch menu on opening day, and in the years since then it's become a staple for the lunch crowd. I first started serving a swordfish club at Mesa Grill years ago, and its popularity prompted me to redesign the sandwich with a more distinctly American feel. Creamy avocado slices add a nice touch of richness to the lean, meaty swordfish. Juicy tomato, peppery watercress, and a fresh lemony mayonnaise complete this vibrant sandwich. Serve with Barbecued Potato Chips (page 163) and pickled carrots and okra if desired.

Serves 4

4 (6-ounce) swordfish fillets
2 tablespoons canola oil
Kosher salt and freshly ground black pepper
8 (½-inch-thick) slices Pullman or other good-
    quality white sandwich bread
Lemon Mayonnaise (recipe follows)
1 ripe Hass avocado, halved, pitted, peeled, and
    each half cut into 6 slices
1 ripe beefsteak tomato, sliced ¼ inch thick
1 bunch of watercress, chopped

1. Preheat the grill to high or heat a grill pan over high heat. Brush the fish on both sides with the oil and season with salt and pepper. Grill until golden brown on both sides and just cooked through, about 4 minutes per side. Remove and let rest for a few minutes.

2. Grill the bread on both sides until lightly golden brown, about 30 seconds per side. Lay the slices of bread on a flat surface and spread each slice with a tablespoon of the mayonnaise. Place a fillet on 4 of the slices of bread and top with 3 slices avocado, 1 slice tomato, and some watercress. Place the remaining slices of bread on top of the watercress, mayonnaise side down.

LEMON MAYONNAISE
Makes ½ cup

½ cup mayonnaise
1 teaspoon finely grated lemon zest
2 teaspoons fresh lemon juice
Kosher salt and freshly ground black pepper

Whisk together the mayonnaise, zest, and juice in a small bowl and season with salt and pepper. Cover and refrigerate for at least 30 minutes before serving to allow the flavors to meld. The lemon mayonnaise can be prepared 1 day in advance and stored covered in the refrigerator.

PULLED BARBECUED DUCK SANDWICH
COLESLAW, SPICY PICKLES

This is an obvious play on the southern pulled
pork sandwich, which is typically made with braised pork
shoulder. Duck legs are an interesting upgrade. While
duck breasts are best cooked quickly and served rare,
the legs need to be slow-cooked to make them tender.
I believe in employing strong flavors such as fresh ginger,
star anise, fennel, and cinnamon to cut through the
richness of duck. The pickles and coleslaw are optional,
but I can't imagine having a pulled pork—or, in this case,
pulled duck—sandwich without them. That crunchy,
vinegary bit of freshness truly rounds out the sandwich.
Serves 4 to 6

Duck

10 skinless duck legs (about 5 pounds)
Kosher salt and freshly ground black pepper
1¼ cups Bar Americain Barbecue Sauce
    (page 236) or store-bought barbecue sauce
3 cups chicken stock, homemade (page 240)
    or store-bought
1 medium red onion, coarsely chopped
1 (2-inch) piece fresh ginger, peeled and chopped
6 cloves
2 star anise
2 cinnamon sticks
½ teaspoon fennel seeds
½ teaspoon black peppercorns

Coleslaw

½ cup mayonnaise
2 tablespoons Dijon mustard
2 tablespoons apple cider vinegar
½ teaspoon celery seeds
½ teaspoon celery salt
½ head napa cabbage, finely shredded
1 large carrot, coarsely grated
1 small red onion, halved and thinly sliced
Kosher salt and freshly ground black pepper

4 to 6 brioche buns, split and lightly toasted
Spicy Pickles (recipe follows; optional)

1. To cook the duck, preheat the oven to 325°F.

2. Heat a grill pan over high heat. Season the duck legs with salt and pepper on both sides and brush with ¾ cup of the barbecue sauce. Grill the legs until golden brown, 3 to 4 minutes on each side.

3. Put the stock in a medium roasting pan, add the remaining ½ cup barbecue sauce, the onion, ginger, cloves, star anise, cinnamon sticks, fennel seeds, and black peppercorns and season with salt. Arrange the duck legs in the pan, cover with foil, and braise in the oven until the meat is tender and falling off the bone, 1½ to 2 hours.

4. Meanwhile, make the coleslaw. Whisk together the mayonnaise, mustard, vinegar, celery seeds, and celery salt in a large bowl. Add the cabbage, carrot, and onion, season with salt and pepper, and toss well to combine. Cover and refrigerate for at least 30 minutes and up to 4 hours before serving.

5. Transfer the duck to a platter and tent loosely with foil. Skim off any fat from the liquid; then strain the liquid into a bowl. Pour 2 cups of the braising liquid into a large sauté pan and boil over high heat until reduced to 1 cup, 8 to 10 minutes. Shred the duck into bite-sized pieces, add to the reduced sauce, and toss to combine.

6. Mound the duck onto the bottoms of the buns, top with some of the coleslaw and a few pickle slices, if desired, and cover with the tops. Serve extra pickles on the side.

SPICY PICKLES
Makes 1 pint

3 cups apple cider vinegar
2 cloves garlic
1 jalapeño chile, thinly sliced
3 tablespoons sugar
2 teaspoons kosher salt
¼ cup finely chopped fresh dill
2 Kirby cucumbers, sliced ¼ inch thick

1. Bring the vinegar, garlic, jalapeño, sugar, and salt to a simmer in a saucepan over high heat and cook until the sugar dissolves, about 1 minute. Remove from the heat, add the dill, and let cool to room temperature.

2. Place the cucumbers in a small container with a lid, pour the vinegar solution over them, and stir to combine. Cover and refrigerate for at least 2 hours and up to 2 days before serving.

CEDAR-PLANKED BURGER
RED WINE BARBECUE SAUCE, CHEDDAR CHEESE, SAUTÉED MUSHROOMS

Cooking over cedar planks creates amazing flavor, infusing every bite with smoky complexity. And so I decided it was time for salmon to share the cedar love and give burgers some of that star treatment. It works. Since this is, after all, a method born in the Pacific Northwest, it only seems right to outfit the burger with toppings inspired by the region. A barbecue sauce made with Pinot Noir—the grape that put Oregon's wine on the map—and an earthy sauté of wild mushrooms flavorfully fit the bill.

Serves 4

2 untreated cedar planks, each about
    5 x 12 inches
2 tablespoons extra virgin olive oil
1½ pounds assorted mushrooms (cremini,
    shiitake caps, morel, oyster), coarsely chopped
2 shallots, thinly sliced
1 tablespoon finely chopped fresh thyme
Kosher salt and freshly ground black pepper
Canola oil, for brushing
1½ pounds ground chuck (80 percent lean)
Red Wine Barbecue Sauce (recipe follows)
8 (⅛-inch-thick) slices aged cheddar cheese
4 hamburger buns, split and warmed

1. Submerge the cedar planks in cold water and soak for at least 1 hour.

2. Preheat the oven to 400°F.

3. Heat the olive oil in a large sauté pan over high heat. Add the mushrooms and cook, stirring occasionally, until they begin to soften, about 5 minutes. Add the shallots and cook until the mushrooms are golden brown, about 5 minutes longer. Stir in the thyme and season with salt and pepper.

4. Remove the planks from the water, put them on a baking sheet, and place them in the oven for 15 minutes. Remove and brush the tops of the planks with canola oil.

5. Raise the oven temperature to 425°F.

6. Divide the meat into 4 equal portions. Form each portion loosely into a ¾-inch-thick burger and then make a deep depression in the center with your thumb. Season both sides of each burger with salt and pepper.

7. Place 2 burgers on each plank, leaving a few inches between the burgers. Brush the tops of the burgers with some of the barbecue sauce and place the planks in the oven. Cook, basting with some of the sauce every few minutes, until the burgers reach the desired doneness, 10 to 12 minutes for medium-rare. Top each burger with 2 slices of cheese during the last minute of cooking.

8. Remove from the oven and top each burger with a large spoonful of the mushrooms. Serve the warm buns on the side.

RED WINE BARBECUE SAUCE
Makes about 1 cup

2 tablespoons olive oil
2 large shallots, coarsely chopped
2 cloves garlic, coarsely chopped
2 tablespoons ground ancho chile
1 tablespoon smoked sweet Spanish paprika
¼ teaspoon ground chile de árbol or cayenne
1 cup dry red wine, such as Pinot Noir
1 cup ketchup
1 heaping tablespoon Dijon mustard
1 tablespoon red wine vinegar
1 tablespoon Worcestershire sauce
1 canned chipotle chile in adobo, chopped
2 tablespoons dark brown sugar
1 tablespoon honey
1 tablespoon molasses
Kosher salt and freshly ground black pepper

1. Heat the oil in a heavy medium saucepan over medium heat. Add the shallots and garlic and cook until soft, 3 to 4 minutes. Add the ground ancho, paprika, and ground chile de árbol and cook for 30 seconds. Raise the heat to high, add the wine, and boil until completely evaporated.

2. Add the ketchup and ½ cup water and bring to a boil. Lower the heat and simmer for 5 minutes. Add the mustard, vinegar, Worcestershire, chipotle, brown sugar, honey, and molasses and simmer, stirring occasionally, until thickened, about 10 minutes.

3. Transfer the mixture to a food processor and puree until smooth. Season with salt and pepper. Pour into a bowl and allow to cool at room temperature. The sauce will keep for 1 week in a tightly sealed container stored in the refrigerator.

GREEN CHILE CHEESEBURGER

Unknown to the majority of this country, the green chile cheeseburger is a beloved culinary treasure of New Mexico. Having been there and sampled my share, I know exactly why New Mexicans love it as they do, and that's why I had to bring my own version to New York. With its fresh bite, the Hatch chile is a favorite in New Mexico, where there is a whole festival celebrating the hometown crop. I like to add some heat to my green chile relish with roasted serranos and use milder, peppery poblano chiles to round out the mix. Tossing the chiles with acidic red wine vinegar and vibrant cilantro ensures a nice freshness to balance the creamy, decadent cheese sauce. Add some bright color and flavor with pickled red onions and some salty crunch with blue tortilla chip crumbles, and you've got a burger worth serving to even the toughest New Mexico critics.

Serves 4

Green Chile Relish

1 medium poblano chile, roasted, peeled, seeded, and thinly sliced (see page 250)

2 Hatch chiles, roasted, peeled, seeded, and thinly sliced (see page 250)

1 serrano chile, roasted, peeled, seeded, and thinly sliced (see page 250)

¼ cup red wine vinegar

1 tablespoon honey

2 tablespoons extra virgin olive oil

3 tablespoons chopped fresh cilantro

Kosher salt and freshly ground black pepper

Burgers

1 tablespoon canola oil

1½ pounds ground chuck (80 percent lean)

4 hamburger buns, split and lightly toasted

Queso Sauce (recipe follows)

Pickled Red Onion (page 117)

12 blue or yellow corn tortilla chips, coarsely crushed

1. To make the relish, combine the poblano, Hatches, serrano, vinegar, honey, olive oil, and cilantro in a bowl and season with salt and pepper. Let sit at room temperature for at least 30 minutes before serving. The relish can be made 1 day in advance and refrigerated; bring to room temperature before serving.

2. To cook the burgers, heat a griddle or a large sauté pan over high heat. Add the canola oil and heat until it begins to shimmer.

3. Divide the meat into 4 equal portions. Form each portion loosely into a ¾-inch-thick burger and then make a deep depression in the center with your thumb. Season both sides of each burger with salt and pepper. Cook the burgers until golden brown on both sides and cooked to medium, about 8 minutes.

4. Place the burgers on the buns and top each with a few tablespoons of the queso sauce, the green chile relish, pickled onion, and chips. Cover with the bun tops.

QUESO SAUCE
Makes 2½ cups

1 tablespoon unsalted butter

1 tablespoon all-purpose flour

1 cup whole milk, or more if needed

¾ pound Chihuahua or Monterey Jack cheese, coarsely grated (about 3 cups)

3 tablespoons freshly grated Parmesan cheese

Kosher salt and freshly ground black pepper

Melt the butter in a small saucepan over medium heat. Whisk in the flour and cook for 1 minute. Add the milk, increase the heat to high, and cook, whisking constantly, until slightly thickened, about 5 minutes. Remove from the heat and whisk in the Chihuahua cheese until melted. Stir in the Parmesan and season with salt and pepper. Thin with additional milk if needed. Keep warm.

BISON REUBEN SANDWICH
HUNDRED ISLAND DRESSING

A trip to New York City wouldn't be complete without stopping in a Jewish-style deli, and you can't go to a New York deli without trying a Reuben sandwich piled sky-high with corned beef brisket, sauerkraut, Swiss cheese, and Russian or Thousand Island dressing. This is my southern take on that great sandwich. Lean bison is naturally lower in fat than beef, but its flavor is quite similar and you should feel free to use beef brisket if you can't find or don't care for bison. I often dress red cabbage as coleslaw for sandwiches, but cooking it first mellows its bitter note. Hundred Island Dressing is revamped from the original with a substitution of pickled okra for pickle relish. Okra reinforces the southern touch that's also present in the barbecue sauce.

Serves 8

Bison

3 cups Bar Americain Barbecue Sauce (page 236) or store-bought barbecue sauce

1 buffalo brisket (about 4 pounds)

2 tablespoons canola oil

Kosher salt and freshly ground black pepper

2 carrots, coarsely chopped

2 medium onions, coarsely chopped

2 stalks celery, coarsely chopped

6 cloves garlic, coarsely chopped

1 quart chicken stock, homemade (page 240) or store-bought

Pickled Red Cabbage

1¼ cups red wine vinegar

3 tablespoons honey

Kosher salt and freshly ground black pepper

1 large head of red cabbage, cored and thinly sliced

16 (¼-inch-thick) slices Pullman or other good-quality white sandwich bread

¼ pound fontina cheese, grated (1 cup)

Hundred Island Dressing (recipe follows)

8 tablespoons (1 stick) unsalted butter

1. Place 2 cups of the barbecue sauce in a large shallow baking dish, add the brisket, and turn to coat. Cover and marinate in the refrigerator for 4 hours or overnight.

2. Preheat the oven to 325°F.

3. Heat the oil in a large Dutch oven over high heat until it begins to shimmer. Remove the brisket from the refrigerator, season with salt and pepper, and sear well on both sides until golden brown, about 5 minutes per side. Transfer to a plate. Add the carrots, onions, and celery and cook until soft and golden brown, about 5 minutes. Add the garlic and cook for 1 minute.

4. Return the brisket to the pan and add the chicken stock and the remaining 1 cup barbecue sauce. Bring to a simmer on top of the stove; then cover and place in the oven. Cook until fork-tender, about 2 hours.

5. Meanwhile, make the pickled red cabbage. Bring the vinegar, honey, and salt and pepper to taste to a simmer in a large Dutch oven over medium heat. Add the cabbage and cook, stirring occasionally, until just wilted, about 15 minutes.

6. Remove the brisket from the cooking liquid, tent with foil, and let rest for 15 minutes before slicing thinly across the grain.

7. Place 8 slices of bread on a work surface. Top each slice with 4 or 5 slices of brisket, 2 tablespoons of the cheese, some pickled red cabbage, and a drizzle of the dressing. Top with the remaining bread.

8. Heat one-third of the butter in a large skillet over medium heat. Cook 2 to 3 sandwiches at a time until golden brown on both sides and the cheese has melted, about 3 minutes per side. Repeat with the remaining butter and sandwiches.

HUNDRED ISLAND DRESSING
Makes about 1½ cups

1 cup mayonnaise
3 tablespoons ketchup
1 to 2 teaspoons Frank's RedHot or other hot sauce, to taste
Kosher salt and freshly ground black pepper
¼ cup finely chopped pickled okra

Whisk together the mayonnaise, ketchup, and hot sauce in a small bowl and season with salt and pepper. Cover and refrigerate for at least 1 hour and up to 1 day. Stir in the pickled okra just before using.

APPETIZERS

HOT POTATO CHIPS
BLUE CHEESE SAUCE

I cannot begin to tell you how addictive these chips and sauce are. Homemade potato chips, crisp and hot from the fryer, dunked in a warm, creamy sauce rich with tangy blue cheese . . . you can't go wrong. Try it for yourself and you'll understand why diners at the restaurant have been known to call over their server and order another round—or two! I like to use an American blue cheese such as Maytag or Great Hill Farms. If you're not up to making your own chips, store-bought ones can be warmed in a 350°F oven for 5 minutes and served with the sauce. When it comes down to it, it's the rich blue cheese sauce that steals the show.

Serves 8

Blue Cheese Sauce
2 cups whole milk, or more if needed

2 tablespoons unsalted butter

1 small Spanish onion, finely chopped

2 tablespoons all-purpose flour

¼ teaspoon kosher salt

Pinch of cayenne

½ pound blue cheese, crumbled, plus ¼ cup for
    garnish

2 tablespoons finely chopped fresh chives,
    for garnish

Potato Chips
4 large Idaho potatoes, peeled and sliced
    lengthwise ⅛ inch thick on a mandoline

2 quarts peanut oil or canola oil

Kosher salt

1. Pour the milk into a small saucepan and bring to a simmer over low heat.

2. Melt the butter in a medium saucepan over medium heat. Add the onion and cook until soft. Stir in the flour and cook for 1 minute. Slowly whisk in the warm milk and continue whisking until thickened, about 2 minutes. Season with the salt and cayenne. Continue cooking for 5 minutes, whisking occasionally. Remove from the heat and stir in the blue cheese. If the sauce is too thick, thin with a little extra milk. Keep warm.

3. Place the potato slices on a baking sheet between layers of paper towels to make sure they are very dry before frying.

4. Heat the oil in a large saucepan over medium heat until it reaches 375°F on a deep-fat thermometer. Fry the potatoes in small batches until golden brown on both sides, turning once, about 2 minutes. Remove with a slotted spoon and place on a brown paper bag or another baking sheet lined with paper towels to drain. Immediately season with salt.

5. Pour the sauce into a bowl and top with the remaining ¼ cup crumbled blue cheese and the chopped chives. Place the bowl in the center of a large platter and arrange the potato chips around the bowl.

OYSTER AND LOBSTER SHOOTERS

Oyster shooters are a fun, tasty cocktail–hors d'oeuvre hybrid. Take a freshly shucked plump oyster, drop it into a shot glass, top off with booze, and tip it back. I started serving them at Bobby Flay Steak, where the mood is festive and the diners are often open to excess. This shooter adds a meaty coin of sweet lobster to the oyster to do the trick! The "shot" part of the dish is a smoky, vodka-spiked cocktail sauce, which is almost like a concentrated Bloody Mary. I thought these would be a perfect addition to the menu at Bar Americain too. I was right.

Serves 8

1 (8-ounce) lobster tail, steamed
8 oysters, shucked
Cocktail Sauce (recipe follows)
Green Tabasco sauce
Grated lime zest

1. Put the lobster tail on a cutting board and cut it crosswise into 8 equal slices.

2. Slip 1 oyster into a double shot glass, top with a slice of lobster, a heaping tablespoon of the cocktail sauce, a splash of green Tabasco sauce, and some lime zest. Repeat with the remaining ingredients and serve immediately.

COCKTAIL SAUCE
Makes about 1 cup

½ cup ketchup
3 tablespoons prepared horseradish, drained
3 tablespoons vodka
1 tablespoon pureed canned chipotle chile
   in adobo
2 teaspoons Worcestershire sauce
Juice of ½ small lemon
Kosher salt and freshly ground black pepper

Whisk together the ketchup, horseradish, vodka, chipotle, Worcestershire, and lemon juice in a small bowl. Season with salt and pepper. Cover and refrigerate for at least 30 minutes and up to 8 hours before serving.

BARBECUED OYSTERS
BLACK PEPPER-TARRAGON BUTTER

There are many people out there who claim to be oyster lovers yet have eaten them only raw. It's true that slurping down an oyster on the half shell is a great culinary experience, but to call yourself a true oyster aficionado you need to open yourself up to the glories of the cooked oyster. The meat is tender and even buttery, its fresh taste of the sea concentrated by the oven's heat. A rich butter seasoned with the soft licoricelike flavor of tarragon and the sharp bite of black pepper melts over the cooked oyster, joining the oyster's juices in the shell. Serving the oyster shells on a bed of salt is both an attractive and a handy presentation; the salt keeps the shells upright and keeps them from sliding around the platter.

Serves 4

8 tablespoons (1 stick) unsalted butter, softened

3 tablespoons fresh tarragon, chopped,
    plus whole leaves for garnish

½ teaspoon coarsely ground black pepper

Kosher salt

1¼ cups Bar Americain Barbecue Sauce
    (page 236) or store-bought barbecue sauce

1 tablespoon ground cascabel chile or
    1 teaspoon cayenne

20 oysters, scrubbed

1. Combine the butter and chopped tarragon in a food processor and process until smooth. Add the black pepper and 1 teaspoon salt and pulse a few times to combine. Scrape the mixture into a bowl.

2. Preheat a grill or the broiler to high or heat a grill pan over high heat. Spread 1 cup kosher salt over the bottom of a large platter.

3. Combine the barbecue sauce and chile powder in a small saucepan and bring to a simmer over low heat. Keep warm.

4. Carefully shuck the oysters over a bowl, reserving all of the oyster liquor. Return each oyster to its bottom shell; discard the top shells. Add some of the oyster liquor back to the oysters in the shell. Top each oyster with about a teaspoon of the butter.

5. Carefully place the oysters in the half shell on the grates of the grill or on the grill pan. Cook until the sauce starts to bubble and the oysters are just cooked through, about 2 minutes. (Alternatively, you can place them on a baking sheet and heat under a preheated broiler for about 2 minutes.)

6. Remove the oysters from the grill using tongs, place on top of the salt on the platter, and top each with a small spoonful of the barbecue sauce. Garnish with tarragon leaves and serve immediately.

SHRIMP-TOMATILLO COCKTAIL

Horseradish is the common link between the ketchup-based cocktail sauce you are used to and this, its Bar Americain reincarnation. Tart tomatillos are roasted and blended with garlic, red onion, jalapeños, and cilantro for a sauce indebted to the flavors of the American Southwest. The secret to its bright green hue is the addition of blanched and chopped spinach—the flavor isn't noticeable, but the color certainly is.

Serves 4 to 6

> 2 tablespoons kosher salt
> 1 tablespoon coriander seeds
> 2 teaspoons black peppercorns
> 2 lemons, quartered
> 1½ pounds large (21 to 24 count) shrimp, peeled and deveined
> Tomatillo-Horseradish Sauce (recipe follows)

1. Fill a medium saucepan with 2 quarts cold water. Add the salt, coriander, peppercorns, and lemon wedges, squeezing the juice into the pot first, and bring to a boil over high heat. Boil for 5 minutes.

2. Turn the heat off, add the shrimp, cover, and let the shrimp sit in the liquid for 15 minutes, to cook through and absorb the flavor. Drain the shrimp in a colander, place in a bowl, cover, and chill in the refrigerator for at least 1 hour and up to 8 hours.

3. Pour the sauce into short glasses or martini glasses and hang the shrimp on the rims of the glasses, tail ends out.

TOMATILLO-HORSERADISH SAUCE
Makes about 2 cups

> 10 tomatillos, husked and rinsed
> 1 medium red onion, coarsely chopped
> 3 cloves garlic
> 2 jalapeño chiles
> 3 tablespoons canola oil
> Kosher salt and freshly ground black pepper
> ½ cup packed fresh spinach leaves
> 3 tablespoons rice wine vinegar
> ¼ cup prepared horseradish, drained
> ¼ cup chopped fresh cilantro
> 1 tablespoon honey

1. Preheat the oven to 375°F.

2. Place the tomatillos, onion, garlic, and jalapeños in a medium roasting pan, toss with the oil, and season with salt and pepper. Roast, stirring occasionally, until the mixture is soft, 25 to 35 minutes.

3. Meanwhile, bring a medium saucepan of salted water to a boil. Have ready a medium bowl filled with ice water. Plunge the spinach into the boiling water and boil for 1 minute. Drain well and transfer to the ice water. Once cool, squeeze out the spinach to remove excess water.

4. Transfer the tomatillo mixture to a food processor, add the spinach, vinegar, horseradish, cilantro, and honey, and pulse until smooth. Season with salt and pepper. Scrape into a bowl, cover, and refrigerate for at least 1 hour and up to 8 hours before serving. Bring to room temperature before serving.

LOBSTER-AVOCADO COCKTAIL

Sharp pickled horseradish, savory Worcestershire sauce, anise-flavored tarragon, and peppery watercress bring a kick to creamy cubes of avocado and rich lobster. We serve this and our other seafood cocktails in glasses so that they can be appreciated from every angle; it's a great way to stretch an expensive ingredient without sacrificing any of its luxurious appeal.

Serves 4

⅓ cup fresh lime juice

2 tablespoons prepared horseradish, drained

2 tablespoons Worcestershire sauce

2 teaspoons honey

1 teaspoon Tabasco sauce

1 tablespoon chopped fresh tarragon

Kosher salt and freshly ground black pepper

1 (2½- to 3-pound) lobster, steamed and meat removed and diced

½ cup chopped watercress

1 ripe avocado, halved, pitted, and diced

Whisk together the lime juice, horseradish, Worcestershire, honey, Tabasco, and tarragon in a medium bowl. Season with salt and pepper. Gently fold in the lobster and watercress. Scoop the avocado from its shell and fold it into the lobster mixture. Divide among 4 martini glasses.

CRAB-COCONUT COCKTAIL

Miami! That's where a bite of this lush crab cocktail takes me. The tropical touch of coconut milk and ripe mango enhances the natural sweetness of lump crabmeat. A good dose of lime juice and a healthy dash of habanero hot sauce keep the dish fresh, not cloying. Salty plantain chips—found at most grocery stores or Latin markets—further boost the Latin vibe.

Serves 4

1 cup canned unsweetened coconut milk

3 tablespoons habanero hot sauce, or more
to taste

Juice of 2 limes

2 tablespoons honey

1 teaspoon kosher salt

¼ teaspoon freshly ground black pepper

1 pound jumbo lump crabmeat, picked over

½ ripe mango, peeled, pitted, and finely diced

½ cup thinly sliced Belgian endive

½ cup thinly sliced radicchio

¼ cup chopped fresh cilantro

1. Whisk together the coconut milk, hot sauce, lime juice, honey, salt, and pepper in a large bowl, cover, and let sit at room temperature for 15 minutes.

2. Gently fold in the crab, mango, endive, radicchio, and cilantro and stir to combine. Using a slotted spoon, divide the mixture among 4 martini glasses.

GULF SHRIMP AND GRITS
BACON, GREEN ONIONS, GARLIC

This is my tip-of-the-hat to the picturesque city of Charleston, South Carolina. Each time I visit I am charmed by the city's citizens, its architecture, and its Low Country cuisine, in particular the sumptuous shrimp and grits. Originally a humble breakfast made by and for the local shrimp fishermen, this dish of creamy grits and plump shrimp deserves a night out on the town. Sharp cheddar cheese and heavy cream enrich the grits with lush flavor. Thick matchsticks of smoky bacon are rendered crisp for a salty garnish, and the flavorful fat is used to sauté the sweet shrimp. Lemony thyme and chopped garlic season the shrimp to savory perfection. **Serves 4**

Grits
4 to 5 cups Shrimp Stock (page 241)
Kosher salt and freshly ground black pepper
1 cup stone-ground yellow cornmeal
¼ pound white cheddar cheese, grated (1 cup)
¼ cup heavy cream
2 green onions, green part only, thinly sliced,
    for garnish

Sautéed Shrimp
½ pound thick-cut double-smoked bacon, cut
    crosswise into ¼-inch strips
20 large (21 to 24 count) shrimp, peeled and
    deveined
Kosher salt and freshly ground black pepper
3 cloves garlic, finely chopped
2 teaspoons chopped fresh thyme

1. To make the grits, bring 4 cups of the shrimp stock and 2 teaspoons salt to a boil in a medium saucepan over high heat. Slowly whisk in the cornmeal and bring to a boil. Reduce the heat to medium and continue cooking, whisking every few minutes, until the grits are soft and have lost their gritty texture, 25 to 30 minutes. If the mixture becomes too thick, add the remaining cup of stock and continue cooking until absorbed. Add the cheese and cream and whisk until smooth. Season with salt and pepper. Keep warm.

2. Cook the bacon in a medium pan over medium heat until golden brown and crisp and the fat has rendered, about 8 minutes. Transfer the bacon with a slotted spoon to a plate lined with paper towels.

3. Spoon off all but 3 tablespoons bacon fat from the pan and return the pan to the stove over high heat. Season the shrimp with salt and pepper. Working in batches if needed, add the shrimp, garlic, and thyme to the pan and sauté until the shrimp are light golden brown on both sides and just cooked through, 1 to 2 minutes per side. Transfer the shrimp to a plate. Reserve the garlic oil left in the pan to drizzle over the finished dish.

4. Divide the grits among 4 shallow bowls and top each with 5 shrimp. Drizzle the shrimp with some of the garlic oil and sprinkle with the bacon and green onions.

RED PEPPER CRAB CAKES
RED CABBAGE SLAW, BASIL VINAIGRETTE

The dominant component of any good crab cake should always be crab—not breading. An extra finely milled flour such as Wondra is the perfect binder; it helps hold the cake together without adding its own texture or flavor to the mix—this is all gorgeous crab. The spicy-sweet tang of roasted piquillo peppers gives these crab cakes a kick of rich flavor. This gorgeous purple slaw, with ribbons of bright green basil running throughout, is slightly sweet and totally fresh. More than a garnish, it delivers crunch and taste that complete the dish.

Makes 8 crab cakes; serves 8 as an appetizer or 4 as a main course

Red Cabbage Slaw

¼ cup fresh orange juice

Juice of 1 lime

¼ cup chopped fresh basil, plus 8 leaves, thinly sliced

1 heaping tablespoon honey

Kosher salt and freshly ground black pepper

½ cup canola oil

½ small head of red cabbage, finely shredded

1 medium carrot, coarsely grated

2 green onions, green and pale green parts, thinly sliced

Crab Cakes

¼ cup plus 1 tablespoon canola oil

3 cloves garlic, finely chopped

½ cup mayonnaise

2 piquillo peppers, drained, or 1 red bell pepper, roasted, peeled, seeded (see page 250), and chopped

3 tablespoons prepared horseradish, drained

¼ teaspoon ground chile de árbol or cayenne

Kosher salt and freshly ground black pepper

1½ pounds jumbo lump crabmeat, picked over

3 green onions, green and pale green parts, thinly sliced

2 to 3 tablespoons Wondra flour

2½ cups panko bread crumbs

Basil Vinaigrette (recipe follows)

Fresh basil sprigs, for garnish

1. To make the red cabbage slaw, combine the orange juice, lime juice, chopped basil, honey, 1 teaspoon salt, and ¼ teaspoon pepper in a blender and blend until smooth. With the motor running, slowly add the oil and blend until emulsified.

2. Put the cabbage, carrot, green onions, and sliced basil leaves in a medium bowl, add the dressing, and toss to coat. Season with salt and pepper. Cover and refrigerate for at least 30 minutes and up to 2 hours before serving.

3. To make the crab cakes, heat 1 tablespoon of the oil in a small sauté pan over medium heat. Add the garlic and cook until soft, 1 to 2 minutes.

4. Put the mayonnaise, piquillo peppers, horseradish, garlic, and chile de árbol in a food processor or blender and blend until smooth. Season with salt and pepper. Transfer the mixture to a bowl, gently fold in the crab, green onions, and enough Wondra to bind the mixture slightly, and season with salt and pepper. Cover and refrigerate for at least 2 hours and up to 8 hours.

5. Spread the panko on a large platter or baking sheet and season with salt and pepper. Remove the crab mixture from the refrigerator and divide into 8 equal patties, each about ½ inch thick. Dredge the cakes on both sides in the panko and place on a platter.

6. Heat the remaining ¼ cup canola oil in a large nonstick sauté pan over high heat until the oil begins to ripple. Sauté the cakes until golden brown on both sides and just cooked through, about 3 minutes per side.

7. Drizzle a little of the basil vinaigrette onto 8 small plates. Top the vinaigrette with a crab cake and top with some of the slaw. Drizzle with more of the vinaigrette and garnish with basil sprigs.

BASIL VINAIGRETTE
Makes about ¾ cup

 1 cup tightly packed chopped fresh basil leaves
 ¼ cup mayonnaise
 3 tablespoons white wine vinegar
 2 teaspoons honey
 Kosher salt

Combine the basil, mayonnaise, vinegar, and ¼ cup water in a blender and blend until smooth. The vinaigrette should be slightly pourable; if too thick to pour, add a little more water. Add the honey, season with salt to taste, and blend for a few more seconds. The vinaigrette can be made 8 hours in advance and stored in a container with a tight-fitting lid in the refrigerator.

MUSSELS AND FRIES AMERICAIN
GREEN CHILE BROTH

One of the most popular seafood dishes in France must be steamed mussels with fries. You will find *moules frites* in every kind of restaurant, from beachside cafés to, yes, Parisian brasseries. The seasonings do of course vary, but the most traditional preparation *(moules marinière)* steams the mussels in a broth of white wine, herbs, and some form of onions and/or garlic. The same ingredients serve as the jumping-off point for the fragrant green chile broth in this dish. Mild in terms of heat but heady with peppery flavor, a puree of roasted poblano chiles bestows the flavorful broth with a south-of-the-border twist that's further enhanced and enriched by creamy coconut milk. Serving these mussels with good crusty bread—as well as the fries—is a must. Once you've finished the succulent mussels and crisp, salty fries, you'll want that bread to sop up every last delicious drop of mouthwatering broth from your bowl.

Serves 4

2 tablespoons olive oil

1 medium Spanish onion, coarsely chopped

4 cloves garlic, coarsely chopped

2 poblano chiles, roasted, peeled, seeded (see page 250), and pureed

2 cups bottled clam juice

1 cup canned unsweetened coconut milk

1 cup fresh spinach leaves

1 to 2 tablespoons honey

Kosher salt and freshly ground black pepper

1 cup dry white wine

2 pounds cultivated black mussels, scrubbed and debearded

¼ cup chopped fresh flat-leaf parsley

Fries Americain (page 164; optional)

1. Heat the oil in a Dutch oven or medium pot over medium heat. Add the onion and cook until soft, about 5 minutes. Add the garlic and cook for 30 seconds. Add the poblano puree and clam juice and simmer, stirring occasionally, until reduced by half, about 10 minutes. Add the coconut milk and simmer until reduced by half, about 5 minutes.

2. Transfer the mixture to a blender, add the spinach and honey, season with salt and pepper, and blend the green chile broth until smooth.

3. Rinse out the pot and return to the stove over high heat. Add the wine, bring to a boil, and reduce by half, 3 minutes. Add the green chile broth and bring to a boil. Stir in the mussels, cover the pot, and cook until the mussels open, 4 to 5 minutes. Discard any that do not open.

4. Add the parsley and season with salt and pepper. Spoon the mussels and broth into bowls and serve with the fries on the side if desired.

GOAT CHEESE AND ONION TART
HERB SALAD

This classic French bistro dish is a delicious way to start
a meal. Just as good at room temperature as it is hot,
it's a versatile appetizer that can be made ahead of time
and even served as cocktail party fare. Thin rings of
onion, caramelized until sweet and golden brown, are
covered with a rich and eggy custard, topped with tangy
crumbles of fresh goat cheese, and baked in a delicate
crust much like a quiche. (In fact, this would also do
very well at brunch!) Home-grown ingredients like local
onions and a good American goat cheese, such as one
from Coach Farm or California's Laura Chenel, steer this
tart from purely French to positively American. A cool
salad of tender mesclun greens, lemony parsley, delicate
chervil, and tarragon is tossed in a bright vinaigrette
made with a reduction of fruity Pinot Noir. Plate the
salad directly atop the tart so that each bite contains a
bit of buttery crust, savory filling, and fresh herbs.

Serves 8

Tart Dough

1¼ cups all-purpose flour, plus more for rolling

½ teaspoon kosher salt

8 tablespoons (1 stick) butter, cut into 1-inch
    pieces, chilled

4 to 6 tablespoons ice water, as needed

Filling

1 tablespoon unsalted butter

1 tablespoon canola oil

2 large onions, halved and thinly sliced

1 tablespoon finely chopped fresh thyme

3 large eggs

3 tablespoons cream cheese, at room
    temperature

1 cup heavy cream

1 teaspoon kosher salt

¼ teaspoon freshly ground black pepper

6 ounces fresh goat cheese, cut into small pieces

Parsley Pesto (page 24)
Herb Salad (recipe follows)

1. To make the tart dough, combine the flour and salt in a food processor and pulse a few times to combine. Scatter the butter over the flour and pulse until the mixture resembles coarse meal, 6 to 8 pulses.

2. With the machine running, add ¼ cup ice water in a slow, steady stream through the feed tube. Pulse until the dough holds together without being wet or sticky. To test, squeeze a small amount together: If it holds together, it is ready. If it is crumbly, add up to 2 tablespoons more ice water, 1 tablespoon at a time. Form the dough into a flat disk, cover with plastic wrap, and refrigerate until cold, at least 1 hour and up to 24 hours.

3. Roll out the dough to a 12-inch round on a floured surface. Transfer to a 9-inch tart pan with a removable bottom. Trim the dough overhang to 1 inch. Fold the overhang in and press it to the sides, forming a double-thick high-standing side. Pierce the crust all over with a fork. Freeze the crust for at least 30 minutes and up to 1 month.

4. Position a rack in the center of the oven and preheat the oven to 400°F.

5. Bake the crust on a baking sheet, piercing with a fork if the crust bubbles up in spots, until light golden brown, about 20 minutes. Remove from the oven, keeping the crust on the baking sheet. Reduce the oven temperature to 350°F.

6. To make the filling, melt the butter with the oil in a large sauté pan over medium-low heat. Stir in the onions and thyme and cook, stirring occasionally, until the onions are soft and caramelized, about 45 minutes. Remove from the heat and let cool slightly.

7. Whisk together the eggs and cream cheese in a medium bowl until smooth; then whisk in the cream, salt, and pepper.

8. Arrange the onions evenly over the bottom of the tart shell. Pour the egg mixture over the onions and scatter the goat cheese over the top. Bake until the sides of the filling are slightly puffed and the center still jiggles slightly, about 40 minutes. Remove the tart from the oven and let cool for at least 15 minutes before serving.

9. Slice the tart, top each wedge with some pesto, and serve with the herb salad.

HERB SALAD
Serves 8

> 1 cup dry red wine, preferably Pinot Noir
> 2 tablespoons red wine vinegar
> 1 tablespoon honey
> Kosher salt and freshly ground black pepper
> 6 tablespoons extra virgin olive oil
> 2 ounces mesclun greens
> ¼ cup fresh chervil leaves
> ¼ cup fresh flat-leaf parsley leaves
> 2 tablespoons coarsely chopped fresh tarragon

1. Bring the wine to a boil in a small saucepan over medium-high heat and cook until thickened and reduced to 3 tablespoons, about 10 minutes. Remove from the heat and let cool slightly.

2. Combine the reduced wine, vinegar, and honey in a blender and blend until smooth. Season with salt and pepper. With the motor running, slowly add the oil and blend until emulsified. The vinaigrette can be made 1 day in advance and refrigerated. Bring to room temperature before serving.

3. Combine the greens, chervil, parsley, and tarragon in a large bowl, drizzle with the vinaigrette, and toss to combine.

OVEN-BAKED PIZZA
DOUBLE-SMOKED BACON, CARAMELIZED ONIONS, TOASTED GARLIC

This devilishly good appetizer is an American translation of the Alsatian tarte flambée. The pizza's thin crust is topped with an unbeatable combination of nutty Gruyère, smoky bits of thick bacon, sweet caramelized onions, toasted slices of garlic, and tangy crème fraîche.

Makes 2 (14-inch) pizzas; serves 4 as an appetizer or 2 as a main course

Pizza Dough
¾ cup warm (110°F) water, or more if needed
1¼ teaspoons active dry yeast
2 tablespoons extra virgin olive oil, plus more for the bowl and brushing the pizza
2 cups bread flour, plus more for kneading
2 teaspoons kosher salt

Toppings
⅓ pound double-smoked bacon, sliced crosswise into ¼-inch pieces
Caramelized Onions (page 154)
¼ pound Gruyère cheese, grated (about 1 cup)
¼ cup crème fraîche
Parsley-Garlic Oil (recipe follows)
Fresh flat-leaf parsley leaves, for garnish
Finely grated lemon zest, for garnish

1. To make the pizza dough, measure ¼ cup of the warm water into a 2-cup measuring cup. Sprinkle in the yeast and let stand until the yeast dissolves and foams, about 5 minutes. Add the remaining ½ cup warm water and the olive oil.

2. Pulse the flour and salt in a food processor to combine. Add the yeast mixture and pulse to combine. If the dough does not readily form into a ball, add another tablespoon or two of warm water and pulse until a ball forms. Process until the dough is smooth and satiny, about 30 seconds longer.

3. Turn the dough onto a lightly floured work surface. Knead by hand with a few strokes to form a smooth, round ball. Put the dough into a large oiled bowl and cover the bowl with a clean dish towel. Let rise until doubled in size, about 1½ hours.

4. In a medium sauté pan over medium heat, cook the bacon, stirring occasionally, until golden brown and crisp, about 8 minutes. Transfer with a slotted spoon to a plate lined with paper towels.

5. Preheat the oven to 450°F at least 30 minutes before baking the pizza. Line 2 rimmed baking sheets with parchment paper.

6. Turn out the dough onto a lightly floured work surface and divide the dough in half. Form each piece into a ball and cover with a damp cloth. Working with one piece of dough at a time, shape the dough on top of the parchment-lined baking sheets into rectangles about 14 x 7 x ¼ inch thick. Lightly prick the surface with a fork and brush each with 1 tablespoon olive oil.

7. Bake the pizzas one at a time on the bottom rack of the oven until light golden brown, about 6 minutes. Divide the onions and cheese over the top of each pizza. Return the pizzas to the oven and bake until the cheese has melted, about 3 minutes.

8. To serve, drizzle with the crème fraîche and some parsley-garlic oil. Top with the bacon, garlic chips, parsley leaves, and lemon zest.

PARSLEY-GARLIC OIL
Makes about 1 cup oil and toasted garlic chips

½ cup canola oil
2 cloves garlic, thinly sliced
1 cup packed fresh flat-leaf parsley leaves
Kosher salt and freshly ground black pepper

1. Heat the oil over medium-low heat. Add the garlic and cook until light golden brown, 3 to 4 minutes. Transfer the garlic with a slotted spoon to a plate lined with paper towels. Let the oil cool.

2. Process the garlic oil and parsley in a blender until smooth. Season with salt and pepper.

CRISPY SQUASH BLOSSOMS
PULLED PORK, BLACK PEPPER VINAIGRETTE

Squash blossoms are a spring delicacy. Coated in rice batter and panfried, they become light, crisp envelopes for a savory mixture of tender shreds of pork braised in barbecue sauce and creamy ricotta cheese. The sharp bite of black pepper is mellowed with honey in a vinaigrette that brightens each sumptuous bite.

Serves 6

Braised Pork

2 tablespoons canola oil

1 (2-pound) boneless pork butt

Kosher salt and freshly ground black pepper

1 large red onion, coarsely chopped

1 cup Bar Americain Barbecue Sauce (page 236) or store-bought barbecue sauce

2½ cups chicken stock, homemade (page 240) or store-bought

¼ cup rice wine vinegar

Squash Blossoms

1½ cups ricotta cheese

Kosher salt and freshly ground black pepper

18 squash blossoms

1 quart canola oil

2 cups rice flour

Black Pepper Vinaigrette (recipe follows)

1. Preheat the oven to 350°F.

2. To braise the pork, heat the oil in a medium roasting pan over high heat. Season the pork on all sides with salt and pepper. Sear in the oil until golden brown on all sides, about 15 minutes. Transfer the pork to a plate.

3. Add the onion to the pan and cook until softened, 4 minutes. Add the barbecue sauce and stock and bring to a simmer. Return the pork to the pan, cover the pan with foil, and braise in the oven until the meat is fork-tender, 1½ to 2 hours. Remove from the oven, uncover, and let the pork cool in the liquid.

4. While the pork is braising, put the ricotta in a strainer lined with cheesecloth set over a bowl and let drain in the refrigerator for at least 2 hours.

5. Drain the pork, reserving the liquid, and shred the meat into bite-sized pieces. Set aside. Put 2 cups of the braising liquid into a large sauté pan over high heat and boil until reduced to 1 cup and slightly thickened, 5 minutes. Add the vinegar and cook for 30 seconds. Stir in the shredded pork. Remove from the heat and let cool slightly.

6. Put the drained ricotta into a large bowl; discard the liquid. Add the pork and season with salt and pepper. Gently fill each squash blossom with the mixture and twist the tops of the blossoms to secure the filling.

7. Heat the oil in large saucepan over medium heat until it reaches 365°F on a deep-fat thermometer.

8. While the oil is heating, whisk together 2 cups cold water and the flour until smooth. Season with salt and let sit for 10 minutes.

9. Dip the squash blossoms in the batter and let any excess batter drip off. Fry the squash blossoms in batches, turning once, until light golden brown, 2 to 3 minutes. Drain on a plate lined with paper towels and sprinkle with salt.

10. Drizzle some of the black pepper vinaigrette in the center of each of 6 dinner plates and place 3 squash blossoms on top for each serving.

BLACK PEPPER VINAIGRETTE
Makes about 1¼ cups

⅓ cup rice wine vinegar

2 heaping tablespoons Dijon mustard

½ teaspoon kosher salt

1 teaspoon coarsely ground black pepper

1 tablespoon honey

¾ cup extra virgin olive oil

Whisk together the vinegar, mustard, salt, pepper, and honey until combined. Slowly whisk in the oil until emulsified.

GOLD CORN JOHNNY CAKES
BARBECUED DUCK, CRANBERRY BUTTER

Native Americans showed the Pilgrims how to cook with maize (corn) and probably taught them to make johnny cake, a dense cornmeal bread whose thick batter is shaped into a flat cake and baked or fried on a griddle. These cakes (basically just fried corn bread) are the perfect vehicle for many toppings. One of my favorites is barbecued duck and cranberry butter. Feel free to make your own cranberry relish, use what's left over from your holiday meal, or purchase a good-quality prepared one.

Serves 4

Barbecued Duck
3 duck legs (1½ pounds), skin removed
Kosher salt and freshly ground black pepper
½ cup Bar Americain Barbecue Sauce
     (page 236) or store-bought barbecue sauce
1 tablespoon canola oil
2 cups chicken stock, homemade (page 240)
     or store-bought
3 tablespoons chopped fresh flat-leaf parsley,
     plus whole leaves for garnish

Johnny Cakes
1 cup all-purpose flour
½ cup plus 1 tablespoon fine yellow or
     white cornmeal
2 tablespoons sugar
2 teaspoons kosher salt
1 tablespoon baking powder
2 large eggs, separated
¾ cup whole milk
2 tablespoons unsalted butter, melted and
     cooled, plus more for panfrying
Cranberry Butter (recipe follows)

1. To cook the duck, preheat the oven to 325°F.

2. Season the duck legs on both sides with salt and pepper and brush with ¼ cup of the barbecue sauce. Heat the oil in a large deep ovenproof pot over high heat until it begins to shimmer. Sear the legs on both sides until golden brown, about

3 minutes per side. Add the remaining ¼ cup barbecue sauce and the chicken stock to the pot and bring to a simmer. Cover and cook in the oven until the meat begins to fall off the bone, about 2 hours.

3. Remove the duck from the braising liquid and set aside to cool slightly. Strain the braising liquid and reserve. When the duck is cool enough to handle, shred the meat into bite-sized pieces and discard the bones.

4. Combine the shredded meat with ½ cup of the reserved braising liquid in a sauté pan over medium heat and warm until heated through. Add the chopped parsley and season with salt and pepper.

5. To make the johnny cakes, reduce the oven temperature to 300°F.

6. Whisk together the flour, cornmeal, sugar, salt, and baking powder in a medium bowl.

7. Whisk the egg yolks and milk together in a medium bowl until combined. Whisk the egg whites in an electric mixer fitted with the whisk attachment until stiff peaks form.

8. Add the egg yolk mixture to the flour mixture and mix until just combined. Gently fold in the egg whites followed by the 2 tablespoons melted butter, mixing until the batter is just smooth. Let rest for 10 minutes.

9. Heat a large nonstick sauté pan or cast-iron pan or griddle over medium-high heat. Brush with some melted butter. Spoon 2 heaping tablespoons of the batter into the pan for each johnny cake and, using a small offset spatula, spread the batter slightly to even out the tops. Cook until light golden brown on each side, about 1½ minutes per side. Transfer to a baking sheet and keep warm in the oven until ready to serve. Repeat with the remaining batter, buttering the pan as needed between batches.

10. Spread some of the cranberry butter over each johnny cake and mound some of the duck on top. Garnish with parsley leaves and a drizzle of the braising liquid.

CRANBERRY BUTTER
Makes ¾ cup

8 tablespoons (1 stick) unsalted butter, softened
¼ cup store-bought cranberry relish
1 tablespoon pure maple syrup
Kosher salt and freshly ground black pepper

Combine the butter, cranberry relish, and maple syrup in a food processor and process until smooth. Season with salt and pepper. Scrape into a bowl, cover, and refrigerate for at least 1 hour to allow the flavors to meld. The cranberry butter can be made 1 day in advance and stored, covered, in the refrigerator. Bring to room temperature before using.

SPICY TUNA TARTARE
CLASSIC GARNISHES

At first glance this appears to be a steak tartare presented just as you would find It in any French bistro. Small mounds of finely chopped egg whites, their creamy yellow yolks, sharp red onion, and salty capers surround a carefully shaped ring of chopped red meat, all ready to be mixed and scooped up with crisp rounds of toast. But instead of minced steak, the star of this tartare is fresh tuna. Smoky chipotle puree and pungent Dijon mustard are blended with smooth olive oil so that they can coat each dice of tuna with flavor. Fresh green onions and delicate shallots contribute a soft onion flavor to the tartare, while the briny capers and fresh parsley add brightness. Delicious as is, the deceptive garnishes are what make this a playful American dish.

Serves 4

Tuna Tartare

2 tablespoons Dijon mustard

1 tablespoon pureed canned chipotle chiles in adobo

3 tablespoons extra virgin olive oil

1 large shallot, finely diced

1 pound fresh tuna, cut into ¼-inch dice

2 green onions, green and pale green parts, thinly sliced

2 tablespoons brined capers, drained

¼ cup finely chopped fresh flat-leaf parsley

Kosher salt and freshly ground black pepper

Garnishes

6 hard-cooked eggs, whites and yolks finely chopped separately

1 tablespoon brined capers, drained

½ small red onion, finely diced

¼ cup finely chopped fresh flat-leaf parsley

12 (¼-inch-thick) slices French or Italian bread, toasted, brushed lightly with olive oil, and halved

1. To make the tartare, whisk together the mustard, chipotle puree, oil, and shallot in a medium bowl. Fold in the tuna, green onions, capers, and parsley until combined. Season with salt and pepper. The tartare can be made only up to 10 minutes before serving.

2. Set a 4-inch ring mold in the center of a large dinner plate and gently pack some of the tartare mixture into the mold, pressing down on the top to make an even layer. Remove the mold and repeat to make 3 more servings. Scatter some of the garnishes over and around each plate. Serve each with 3 slices of toast.

STEAK TARTARE
MUSTARD SAUCE, CORNICHONS, GARLIC TOAST

Those of you who love steak tartare—and there seems to be very little middle ground between those who do and those who don't—will be positively enamored of this dish. This is a time when the quality of your ingredients is paramount—purchase the filet from a butcher whom you trust to give you the best selection as opposed to something prewrapped in the market. The egg for the mustard sauce must also be as fresh as possible as it is used raw. Savory anchovies add an extra layer of flavor to the creamy sauce, which pops with whole grain mustard. Crunchy, acidic cornichons, fresh jalapeño—an American touch—and shallots inject the lush tartare with flavor and texture.

Serves 4

1¼ pounds filet mignon
2 tablespoons Dijon mustard
3 tablespoons extra virgin olive oil
1 jalapeño chile, finely diced
1 large shallot, finely diced
6 cornichons, finely diced
2 tablespoons brined capers, drained
3 green onions, green and pale green parts,
  thinly sliced
¼ cup finely chopped fresh flat-leaf parsley
Kosher salt and freshly ground black pepper
Mustard Sauce (recipe follows)
Garlic Toast (recipe follows)

1. Put the beef on a plate and place in the freezer for 15 minutes (this will make dicing the beef easier).

2. Whisk together the mustard and oil in a large bowl. Add the jalapeño, shallot, cornichons, and capers and mix to combine.

3. Remove the meat from the freezer and cut into ¼-inch dice. Put the steak in the bowl with the jalapeño mixture, add the green onions and parsley, and fold gently to combine. Season with salt and pepper.

4. Divide the tartare among 4 large dinner plates, drizzle with some of the mustard sauce, and serve with 3 slices of the garlic toast. Serve immediately.

MUSTARD SAUCE
Makes about 1 cup

1 large egg yolk
2 anchovies in oil, patted dry
1 tablespoon Dijon mustard
1 tablespoon whole grain mustard
2 tablespoons red wine vinegar
¾ cup extra virgin olive oil
Kosher salt and freshly ground black pepper

1. Combine the egg yolk, anchovies, both mustards, and the vinegar in a blender and blend until smooth.

2. With the motor running, slowly add the oil, drop by drop at first, and blend until emulsified. Season with salt and pepper. Cover and refrigerate for at least 1 hour and up to 1 day before serving.

GARLIC TOAST
Makes 12 pieces

2 cloves garlic
½ cup extra virgin olive oil
Kosher salt and freshly ground black pepper
6 (¼-inch-thick) slices Italian bread

1. Preheat the broiler or heat a grill pan over high heat.

2. Combine garlic and oil in a blender and blend for 1 minute. Season with salt and pepper. Pour the mixture into a bowl.

3. Brush both sides of the bread with the garlic oil and broil or grill the bread until lightly golden brown on both sides, about 30 seconds per side. Cut each slice in half. The garlic toasts are best served warm, the day they are made.

FISH AND SHELLFISH

BLACKENED SEA SCALLOPS
GREEN ONIONS, ROASTED TOMATOES

The legendary Louisiana chef Paul Prudhomme started the blackening craze; the method calls for coating seafood or meat in a spice mixture before cooking it in a cast-iron pan. The quick cooking over high heat really seals in flavor as it creates a fantastically flavored blackened crust. Redfish is the traditional choice, but I like the juxtaposition of the spicy rub against the sweetness of scallops. Their meaty richness really holds up well to the aggressive blackening. A simple vinaigrette of green onions adds a vibrant freshness to the dish, as does the smoky tomato relish.

Serves 4

Roasted Tomato Relish

4 ripe plum tomatoes, roasted (see page 108), halved, seeded, and diced

½ small red onion, thinly sliced

2 green onions, green part only, thinly sliced, plus more for garnish

3 tablespoons red wine vinegar

¼ cup extra virgin olive oil

Kosher salt and freshly ground black pepper

Sea Scallops

3 tablespoons smoked sweet Spanish paprika

1 tablespoon ground ancho chile

1 tablespoon ground pasilla chile

1 teaspoon freshly ground white pepper

1 teaspoon freshly ground black pepper

½ teaspoon dried thyme

½ teaspoon dried oregano

¼ teaspoon onion powder

¼ teaspoon garlic powder

¼ teaspoon celery salt

20 U-10 sea scallops, muscle removed

¼ cup canola oil

Kosher salt

Green Onion Vinaigrette (recipe follows)

1. To make the tomato relish, put the tomatoes, red onion, green onions, vinegar, and olive oil in a medium bowl and mix gently to combine. Season with salt and pepper.

2. To cook the sea scallops, combine the paprika, ancho and pasilla powders, white and black pepper, thyme, oregano, onion and garlic powders, and celery salt in a medium shallow bowl.

3. Heat a large cast-iron pan over high heat until it begins to smoke. Brush the scallops on both sides with the oil and season with salt. Dredge one side of each scallop in the spice rub and put the scallops in the pan spice side down. Cook until browned and a crust has formed, 1½ to 2 minutes. Turn the scallops over and continue to cook until just cooked through, 2 to 3 minutes longer.

4. Divide the scallops among 4 large dinner plates, top each scallop with some of the tomato relish, drizzle with the vinaigrette, and sprinkle some green onion on top.

GREEN ONION VINAIGRETTE
Makes about ⅔ cup

¼ cup white wine vinegar

1 small shallot, chopped

2 tablespoons mayonnaise

1 tablespoon honey

6 green onions, green part only, chopped

Kosher salt and freshly ground black pepper

Combine the vinegar, ¼ cup water, the shallot, mayonnaise, and honey in a blender and blend until combined. Add the green onions and blend until smooth. Season with salt and pepper. The vinaigrette can be prepared 4 hours in advance and stored covered in the refrigerator. Bring to room temperature before serving.

CRISPY SOFT SHELL CRABS
LEMON-DILL BROWN BUTTER, SUCCOTASH

Soft shell crab season is short and sweet. When it's here, you want to make the most of it. Highlighting the flavor of the crab is what matters, and I employ a secret weapon to help me do just that. Wondra flour is a super-finely milled ("instant") flour that creates a very thin, almost stealthlike coating around the crabs. What you taste is crisp soft shell crab unadulterated by any thick batter. Simply hit some nutty browned butter with tart lemon juice and anise-flavored dill (an herb that I think is too often forgotten) for an easy and delicious sauce.

Soft shell crabs make their appearance in summer, so it's only fitting to pair them with some of summer's best: fresh lima beans, beefsteak tomatoes (I like local Jersey tomatoes, myself), and of course, corn. This succotash recipe should be considered a guide; try it with whichever fresh vegetables catch your eye at the market.

Serves 4

Succotash
2 tablespoons unsalted butter
1 tablespoon canola oil
1 small Spanish onion, finely diced
1 small red bell pepper, finely diced
2 cloves garlic, finely chopped
1 cup fresh or frozen corn kernels
1 cup drained canned black-eyed peas, rinsed and drained again
1 cup fresh or frozen lima beans, blanched (see page 249)
1 ripe beefsteak tomato, halved, seeded, and diced
Kosher salt and freshly ground black pepper
Finely grated zest of 1 lemon
2 green onions, green and white parts, thinly sliced
¼ cup chopped fresh flat-leaf parsley

Soft Shell Crabs
¾ cup Wondra flour
Kosher salt and freshly ground black pepper

8 medium soft shell crabs, cleaned
8 tablespoons canola oil
10 tablespoons (1¼ sticks) unsalted butter
1 teaspoon finely grated lemon zest
Juice of 1 lemon
3 tablespoons chopped fresh dill

1. To make the succotash, combine the butter and oil in a large sauté pan over high heat and cook until the butter is melted and begins to sizzle. Add the onion and red pepper and cook until soft, about 4 minutes. Add the garlic and cook for 30 seconds. Stir in the corn and cook for 2 minutes.

2. Add the black-eyed peas, lima beans, and tomato, season with salt and pepper, and cook until the tomato softens slightly and the peas and beans are heated through, about 4 minutes.

3. Remove from the heat and stir in the lemon zest, green onions, and parsley. Keep warm.

4. To cook the soft shell crabs, put the flour in a large shallow bowl and season with salt and pepper. Pat the crabs dry with paper towels and season with salt and pepper on both sides.

5. Heat 2 tablespoons of the oil in a large sauté pan over high heat until the oil begins to shimmer. Dredge 2 of the crabs on both sides in the flour and tap off the excess. Place the crabs in the pan, upside down, and cook on each side until golden brown and just cooked through, about 7 minutes total. Wipe the pan out with paper towels and repeat with the remaining oil and crabs. Place 2 crabs on each of 4 plates and tent loosely to keep warm.

6. Wipe out the pan with paper towels and return to the stove over medium heat. Add the butter and cook until it begins to turn a medium brown color, about 3 minutes. Remove from the heat, immediately add the lemon zest and juice and dill, and season with salt and pepper.

7. Pour the sauce over the soft shell crabs and serve the succotash on the side.

RED SNAPPER
CABBAGE SLAW, SALSAS, FLOUR TORTILLAS

Fish tacos originated in Mexico's Baja California and spread up the coast to southern California. Versions featuring deep-fried fish are the most common, but I prefer to grill light, flaky red snapper for these tacos. The grill gives the fish a touch of smoky, charred flavor, which balances the fresh garnishes of tart tomatillo-avocado relish and crunchy red cabbage slaw. Cabbage is a traditional garnish for fish tacos and keeps its crunch factor long past the point when lettuce would have wilted. I make my slaw from a mix of delicate, pale green napa and deep purple red cabbages. Sweet basil may seem an unexpected choice, but its flavor complements the citrus juice in the slaw's vinaigrette and offsets the assertive cilantro in the charred tomato salsa.

Serves 4

Cabbage Slaw
¼ cup fresh lemon juice
¼ cup fresh orange juice
2 tablespoons Dijon mustard
2 tablespoons clover honey
¼ cup fresh basil leaves, chopped
Kosher salt and freshly ground black pepper
½ cup canola oil
2 cups finely shredded napa cabbage
2 cups finely shredded red cabbage
1 large carrot, finely shredded

Fish Tacos
3 (8-ounce) skinless red snapper fillets
Canola oil
Kosher salt and freshly ground black pepper
12 (4-inch) flour tortillas
Charred Tomato Salsa (page 108)
Tomatillo-Avocado Relish (page 108)
Fresh cilantro leaves, for garnish

1. To make the cabbage slaw, put the lemon juice, orange juice, mustard, honey, and basil in a blender and blend until smooth. Season with salt and pepper. With the motor running, add the oil and blend until emulsified. Reserve ¼ cup of the citrus vinaigrette for the fish.

2. Combine the napa and red cabbages and carrot in a large bowl, add the remaining vinaigrette, and toss to coat. Season with salt and pepper. The slaw can be made 1 hour in advance and stored covered in the refrigerator.

3. To cook the fish, preheat the grill to high or heat a grill pan over high heat. Brush both sides of the fish with oil and season with salt and pepper. Grill until golden brown and slightly charred on both sides and just cooked through, about 4 minutes per side. Transfer to a plate and immediately drizzle with the ¼ cup reserved citrus vinaigrette. Let cool slightly and then flake into large pieces using a fork.

4. Grill the tortillas for about 5 seconds per side, until slightly charred. Place the tortillas on a flat surface, fill the center of each with some of the fish, slaw, salsa, relish, and cilantro leaves. Serve 3 tacos per person.

CHARRED TOMATO SALSA
Makes about ¾ cup

4 plum tomatoes
4 tablespoons canola oil
Kosher salt and freshly ground black pepper
1 small red onion, coarsely chopped
3 cloves garlic, chopped
2 teaspoons red wine vinegar
¼ cup chopped fresh cilantro
2 teaspoons honey

1. Preheat the broiler or heat a grill pan over high heat. Brush the tomatoes with 2 tablespoons of the oil and season with salt and pepper. Broil or grill, turning a few times, until the entire surface is blackened, about 5 minutes. Remove and let cool slightly. Slice in half, remove the seeds, and transfer the tomatoes to the bowl of a food processor.

2. Heat the remaining 2 tablespoons oil in a medium sauté pan over high heat. Add the onion and cook until soft, about 4 minutes. Add the garlic and cook for 30 seconds. Add to the tomatoes in the food processor along with the vinegar and process until smooth. Add the cilantro and honey, season with salt and pepper, and pulse a few times. Scrape the mixture into a bowl. Serve at room temperature.

TOMATILLO-AVOCADO RELISH
Makes about 2½ cups

2 ripe Hass avocados, halved, pitted, peeled, and diced
2 tomatillos, husked, rinsed, and diced
Juice of 2 limes
2 tablespoons canola oil
¼ cup chopped fresh cilantro
Kosher salt and freshly ground black pepper

Combine the avocados, tomatillos, lime juice, oil, and cilantro in a medium bowl and season with salt and pepper. The relish is best made just before serving.

CEDAR-PLANKED SALMON
PINOT NOIR REDUCTION, PINOT BUTTER

This dish Is a celebration of the Pacific Northwest's Native American heritage. Native Americans were the first to cook salmon in this way, slowly roasting the dense flesh on cedar planks arranged around an open fire. (You can get the planks at a hardware store.) A light smoky essence permeates the fish as it cooks, boosting the flavor quotient of rich salmon. In addition to the salmon that run though its waters, the Pacific Northwest is known for its lush and balanced Pinot Noir wine. A reduction of the wine is the basis of a darkly fruity, savory sauce that finishes the dish.

Serves 4

Cedar-Planked Salmon
2 untreated cedar planks, each about
    5 x 12 inches
Olive oil
4 (8-ounce) skin-on salmon fillets
Kosher salt and freshly ground black pepper
Pinot Butter (recipe follows)
Fresh flat-leaf parsley leaves, for garnish

Pinot Noir Reduction
3½ cups chicken stock, homemade (page 240)
    or store-bought
6 black peppercorns
2 tablespoons unsalted butter
1 small Spanish onion, chopped
1¼ cups Pinot Noir or other dry red wine
5 sprigs fresh thyme
3 tablespoons honey
Kosher salt and freshly ground black pepper

1. Submerge the cedar planks in cold water and soak for at least 1 hour.

2. Preheat the oven to 400°F.

3. To make the Pinot Noir reduction, combine the stock and peppercorns in a small saucepan and boil over high heat until reduced by half, about 10 minutes.

4. Melt the butter in a medium saucepan over high heat. Add the onion and cook until soft, about 4 minutes. Add the wine, thyme, and 2 tablespoons of the honey and boil until reduced by half, about 7 minutes. Add the reduced stock and boil until reduced by half again, about 5 minutes. Strain the mixture into a clean saucepan and set aside.

5. Remove the planks from the water, put them on a baking sheet, and place them in the oven for 15 minutes. Remove and brush the tops of the planks with olive oil.

6. Brush both sides of the salmon fillets with oil and season with salt and pepper. Place 2 fillets on each plank, leaving a few inches of space between the pieces of fish. Return the planks to the oven and cook the salmon to medium, 10 to 12 minutes.

7. While the salmon is cooking, finish the sauce. Return the saucepan to high heat. Add the remaining 1 tablespoon honey, season with salt and pepper, and cook to a sauce consistency (see page 250); you will have about 1 cup.

8. Transfer the fillets to a platter or immediately serve directly from the planks. Top each fillet with some of the Pinot butter and drizzle with the sauce. Garnish with parsley leaves.

PINOT BUTTER
Makes about ¾ cup

2 cups Pinot Noir
2 tablespoons pure maple syrup
8 tablespoons (1 stick) unsalted butter, softened
Kosher salt and freshly ground black pepper

1. Pour the wine into a small saucepan, bring to a boil over high heat, and cook until reduced to ¼ cup, about 5 minutes. Stir in the maple syrup and let cool.

2. Put the butter in a bowl, add the wine reduction, and stir until combined. Season with salt and pepper. Cover and refrigerate for at least 30 minutes and up to 2 days to allow the flavors to meld.

RED SNAPPER FLORIDA STYLE

Florida, and in particular the city of Miami, has been home to the vibrant culture of Cuban immigrants for generations. Their cuisine has put its stamp on the state and on this dish, where black beans, flavored with chipotle, are pureed into an earthy, slightly chunky sauce that makes the bed for red snapper fillets encrusted in a crisp shell of green plantains. Cool and spicy jalapeño crema and a relish of sweet mango and creamy avocado garnish the fish with tropical continuity.

Serves 4

Black Bean Sauce

1½ cups dried black beans, picked over

1 small red onion, coarsely chopped

2 cloves garlic

2 canned chipotle chiles in adobo, chopped

1 teaspoon ground cumin

Kosher salt

Snapper

4 (6-ounce) red snapper fillets

2 tablespoons canola oil

Kosher salt and freshly ground black pepper

1 green plantain, peeled and sliced paper-thin on a mandoline

Jalapeño Crema (recipe follows)

Mango-Avocado Relish (recipe follows)

Chive Oil (page 239; optional), for garnish

1. To make the black bean sauce, cover the beans by at least 2 inches with cold water and let soak for at least 8 hours or overnight.

2. Drain the beans, place in a medium saucepan, and add the onion, garlic, chipotles, and cumin. Pour in enough cold water to cover by an inch. Bring to a boil, reduce the heat, and simmer, adding more water if the beans appear dry, until the beans are tender, 1 to 1½ hours.

3. Using a slotted spoon, transfer the bean mixture to a food processor. Add 1 cup of the cooking liquid, season with salt, and process until almost smooth; the sauce should be a little chunky. If the sauce is too thick, thin with more of the cooking liquid.

4. To cook the fish, brush the skin side of the snapper with oil and season all over with salt and pepper. Cover the surface of the fish with plantain slices, overlapping them. Brush the plantains with oil and season with salt and pepper.

5. Heat the 2 tablespoons oil in a large nonstick pan over medium-high heat and carefully place the fish in the pan, plantain side down. Cook until the crust is light golden brown, about 4 minutes. Turn the fish over and continue cooking until just cooked through, about 4 minutes longer.

6. Spoon some of the black bean sauce onto 4 plates and drizzle with some of the jalapeño crema. Set the salmon, plantain side up, on top. Spoon some mango-avocado relish next to the fish and garnish with chive oil, if desired.

MANGO-AVOCADO RELISH
Makes about 2 cups

Juice of 2 limes

1 tablespoon canola oil

1 tablespoon honey

Kosher salt and freshly ground black pepper

1 ripe Hass avocado, peeled, pitted, and diced

½ ripe mango, peeled, pitted, and diced

½ small red onion, finely diced

⅓ cup coarsely chopped fresh cilantro

Whisk together the lime juice, oil, and honey in a medium bowl. Season with salt and pepper. Add the avocado, mango, red onion, and cilantro and mix gently to combine. The relish can be made 30 minutes in advance and kept at room temperature.

JALAPEÑO CREMA
Makes ½ cup

½ cup crème fraîche or sour cream
1 large jalapeño chile, roasted, peeled, and
    seeded (see page 250)
Kosher salt and freshly ground black pepper

Combine the crème fraîche and jalapeño in a food
processor and process until smooth. Season with
salt and pepper. Cover and refrigerate for at least
30 minutes and up to 1 day before serving.

SKATE
SMOKED CHILE BUTTER, CAPERS, TARRAGON, CRISPY HOMINY

Skate, for those of you who are unfamiliar with it, is delicately textured and tastes very much like scallops. In France there are endless wonderful brasseries, and nearly all of them serve skate with a brown butter sauce. Smoky chipotle puree instantly Americanizes the butter sauce with its fiery taste of the Southwest. The finishing touches for the skate—salty capers, tart lemon juice, and my favorite herb for seafood, tarragon—are all simple but come together in a dynamic way. The tomato salad is optional, but it brings a lovely touch of bright color and freshness to the plate.

Serves 4

Crispy Hominy
Nonstick cooking spray
1 cup fine white cornmeal, plus 1½ cups
    for dredging
¼ cup freshly grated Parmesan cheese
1 tablespoon unsalted butter, chilled
Kosher salt and freshly ground black pepper
1 cup ricotta cheese
½ cup canola oil

Skate
4 (7 ounce) boneless skate fillets
Kosher salt and freshly ground black pepper
1 cup Wondra flour
3 tablespoons olive oil
½ cup dry white wine
Smoked Chile Butter (page 116)
2 tablespoons brined capers, drained
2 tablespoons fresh lemon juice
2 tablespoons chopped fresh tarragon
Tomato Salad (page 116; optional)
Chive Oil (page 239; optional)

1. To make the crispy hominy, line a baking sheet with parchment paper and spray with nonstick cooking spray.

2. Bring 3 cups water to a boil in a medium saucepan over high heat. Add the cornmeal a little a time, whisking constantly with a wire whisk. Once all the cornmeal has been added, turn the heat to low and cover the pot. Stir the mixture using a wooden spoon every 5 minutes and continue cooking until all the liquid is absorbed and the mixture is very creamy, 25 to 30 minutes.

3. Remove from the heat and stir in the Parmesan and butter and season with salt and pepper. Fold in the ricotta; it does not need to be totally mixed in. Spread the mixture evenly onto the prepared baking sheet to a thickness of ½ inch. Cover with plastic wrap, pressing the wrap into the hominy, and refrigerate until firm, at least 2 hours or overnight.

4. Preheat the oven to 300°F.

5. Spread the 1½ cups of cornmeal on a large plate and season with salt and pepper. Cut the hominy into eight 2-inch rounds. Dredge each cake on both sides in the cornmeal. Heat ¼ cup of the oil in a 9-inch cast-iron pan or a deep sauté pan over medium high heat until the oil begins to shimmer. Sauté 4 of the cakes until golden brown on each side, 1½ to 2 minutes per side. Drain on a plate lined with paper towels and season with salt and pepper. Repeat with the remaining oil and cakes. Transfer to the oven to keep warm while you cook the skate.

6. Season both sides of the skate with salt and pepper. Spread out the flour on a large plate and season with salt and pepper. Dredge the skate on both sides in the flour and tap off any excess.

7. Heat the olive oil in a large nonstick sauté pan over high heat. Cook the skate on both sides until light golden brown and just cooked through, 2 to 3 minutes per side. Transfer to a plate.

(recipe continues)

8. Add the wine to the pan and boil until reduced by half. Remove from the heat. Whisk in the cold chile butter a few tablespoons at a time and whisk until emulsified. Add the capers, lemon juice, and tarragon and season with salt and pepper to taste.

9. Put the fish fillets on 4 plates and serve 2 hominy cakes per person. Spoon the sauce over the fish and top with some of the tomato salad if you like. Garnish with chive oil if desired.

SMOKED CHILE BUTTER
Makes ¾ cup

10 tablespoons (1¼ sticks) unsalted butter, softened
2 tablespoons pureed canned chipotle chiles in adobo
2 teaspoons honey
Kosher salt and freshly ground black pepper

Combine the butter, chipotle puree, and honey in a food processor and blend until smooth. Season with salt and pepper. Scrape into a bowl, cover, and refrigerate for at least 1 hour and up to 2 days.

TOMATO SALAD
Serves 4 as a garnish

1 cup grape tomatoes, sliced in half lengthwise
½ small red onion, thinly sliced
2 tablespoons red wine vinegar
2 tablespoons extra virgin olive oil
2 tablespoons thinly sliced fresh basil
Kosher salt and freshly ground black pepper

Combine the tomatoes, onion, vinegar, oil, and basil in a medium bowl. Season with salt and pepper. Let sit at room temperature for 15 minutes before serving.

PACIFIC COAST BUTTERFISH
SOUR ORANGE GLAZE, PICKLED RED ONION

Butterfish is so named on account of its rich—yes, buttery—flavor. Also known as Pacific pompano, its texture is tender, so long as you don't overcook the fish. (There is an Atlantic pompano as well, but it is much smaller and is not a suitable substitute.) The sour orange glaze is influenced by Cuban cuisine and can be made with either sour oranges or a mixture of sweet orange and lime juices. It's a highly flavorful sauce and a perfect match for the rich fish. I find that the majority of seafood dishes are best suited to the warm weather months and don't fit well into the heartier menus of fall and winter. This assertively flavored dish is an exception to that rule and pairs well with the ingredients and sides of the cool seasons, such as the tender Roasted Brussels Sprouts, Pomegranate, Hazelnuts (page 177) I serve with it at the restaurant.

Serves 4

2 cups fresh orange juice
½ cup fresh lime juice
1 tablespoon white wine vinegar
1½ tablespoons honey
Kosher salt and freshly ground black pepper
2 tablespoons canola oil
4 (8-ounce) butterfish or halibut fillets
Chive Oil (page 239; optional)
Pickled Red Onion (recipe follows)

1. Combine the orange juice and lime juice in a small nonreactive saucepan over high heat and boil until reduced to ⅔ cup, about 8 minutes. Whisk in the vinegar and honey and season with salt and pepper. Let cool slightly. Set aside.

2. Heat the oil in a large nonstick sauté pan over high heat until the oil begins to shimmer. Season the fish on both sides with salt and pepper. Spoon a few tablespoons of the orange glaze into a small bowl. Brush the tops of the fillets with some of the glaze from the small bowl. Put the fillets in the pan, glaze side down, and cook until light golden brown, 3 to 4 minutes. Brush the tops of the fillets with some of the glaze, flip over, and continue cooking until the bottom is light golden brown and the fish is just cooked through, about 4 minutes longer.

3. Place the fillets on 4 large dinner plates and drizzle with a little of the reserved sour orange glaze. Drizzle some of the chive oil, if using, around the plate. Top the fillets with some of the pickled red onion.

PICKLED RED ONION
Makes 1½ cups

1½ cups red wine vinegar
2 tablespoons sugar
1 tablespoon kosher salt
1 medium red onion, halved and thinly sliced

1. Bring the vinegar, ¼ cup water, the sugar, and the salt to a boil in a small saucepan. Remove from the heat and let cool for 10 minutes.

2. Put the onion in a medium bowl, pour the vinegar over, cover, and refrigerate for at least 4 hours and up to 2 days before serving.

WILD STRIPED BASS MONTAUK STYLE
CORN, LOBSTER BROTH, CLAMS

Montauk is a town at the easternmost tip of New York's Long Island, and its waters are a veritable playground for both commercial and weekend fishermen. Wild striped bass practically jump into their boats, and from there it's a short journey to the plates of appreciative diners. This dish is my salute to those responsible for the freshest fish around. Along with briny clams and succulent lobster from its waters, Montauk is home to some spectacular roadside stands and farmers' markets, where in summer you'll find sweet corn and juicy tomatoes.

Serves 4

Lobster Broth
1 tablespoon canola oil
2 small shallots, finely diced
¼ cup brandy
¼ cup sherry
3 cups Lobster Stock (page 240)
20 clams (such as littlenecks or cherrystones), scrubbed
¾ cup fresh or frozen corn kernels
½ cup heavy cream
¼ cup chopped fresh flat-leaf parsley
1 tablespoon finely chopped fresh tarragon, plus whole leaves, for garnish
Kosher salt and freshly ground black pepper

Striped Bass
2 tablespoons canola oil
4 (6-ounce) wild striped bass fillets
Kosher salt and freshly ground black pepper
Fresh flat-leaf parsley sprigs, for garnish

1. Preheat the oven to 400°F.

2. To make the lobster broth, heat the oil in a medium saucepan over medium heat. Add the shallots and cook until soft, about 4 minutes. Increase the heat to high, add the brandy and sherry, and boil until completely evaporated, about 4 minutes.

3. Add the lobster stock and boil, stirring occasionally, until reduced by half, about 7 minutes. Add the clams, cover the pan, and cook until the clams open, 4 to 8 minutes. Transfer the clams with a slotted spoon to a bowl and keep warm. Discard any clams that do not open.

4. Add the corn and cook for 2 minutes. Add the cream and cook until just heated through and slightly reduced, about 2 minutes. Stir in the parsley and tarragon and season with salt and pepper. Keep warm.

5. To cook the fish, heat the oil in a large ovenproof nonstick sauté pan over high heat until it begins to ripple. Season the bass on both sides with salt and pepper. Place the bass in the pan, skin side down, and cook until golden brown, about 3 minutes. Turn the fish over, transfer the pan to the oven, and cook until just cooked through, about 4 minutes.

6. Put a fillet in the center of each of 4 large shallow bowls, skin side up, divide the clams among them, arranging them around the fish, and ladle some of the broth over the fish and clams. Garnish with tarragon leaves.

CORNMEAL-CRUSTED TROUT
CRAWFISH SAUCE

This dish is Louisiana all the way: Crawfish are eaten in other states, to be sure, but no one is as passionate about these crustaceans as are Louisianans. And rightfully so; the state is responsible for producing more than 80 percent of the world's crawfish! Crawfish look like tiny, clawless lobsters, and though they are not directly related, their taste is similar. The lobster stock in the rich, creamy sauce enhances that similarity. Sweet trout fillets get an old-fashioned cornmeal crust and are panfried to a light golden brown before being set down on a pool of the pink sauce.

Serves 4

Crawfish Sauce
2 cups Lobster Stock (page 240)
2 tablespoons tomato paste
1¼ cups heavy cream
½ pound shelled crawfish tails, chopped
1 cup coarsely chopped watercress leaves
Kosher salt and freshly ground black pepper

Trout
1 cup all-purpose flour
Kosher salt and freshly ground black pepper
2 large eggs
2 cups fine yellow cornmeal
4 (8-ounce) trout fillets
4 tablespoons (½ stick) unsalted butter
4 tablespoons canola oil
Watercress leaves, for garnish

1. To make the crawfish sauce, put the lobster stock and tomato paste in a small saucepan and boil over high heat until reduced by half, about 6 minutes.

2. Pour the cream into a medium saucepan and boil over medium heat until reduced by half, about 5 minutes.

3. Meanwhile, to make the trout, spread out the flour on a large plate and season with salt and pepper. Place the eggs in a large shallow bowl. Add a few tablespoons of water, season with salt and pepper, and whisk until combined. Place the cornmeal on a large plate and season with salt and pepper.

4. Add the reduced cream to the lobster stock and stir to combine. Add the crawfish tails and watercress leaves, season with salt and pepper, and cook for 1 to 2 minutes, just to heat through. Keep warm.

5. Season both sides of each fillet with salt and pepper. Dredge one side of each fillet in the flour and tap off any excess, then dip that side in the egg mixture and let any extra drip off. Finally dredge the same side in the cornmeal and tap off any excess.

6. Heat 2 tablespoons of the butter and 2 tablespoons of the oil in a large nonstick sauté pan over high heat until the oil begins to shimmer. Place 2 of the fillets in the pan, cornmeal side down, and cook until golden brown, 2 to 3 minutes. Turn over and continue cooking until just cooked through, 2 to 3 minutes. Repeat with the remaining 2 fillets, butter, and oil.

7. Ladle some of the sauce onto large plates or shallow bowls and top with the trout. Garnish with watercress leaves.

POULTRY AND MEAT

CHICKEN CUTLET ♦ AMERICAN TRIPLE CREAM CHEESE, SOUTHERN HAM, ARUGULA	125
SMOKED CHICKEN ♦ HATCH GREEN CHILE SPOONBREAD, BLACK PEPPER VINEGAR SAUCE	126
SMOKED CHICKEN POT PIE ♦ SWEET POTATO CRUST	128
BUTTERMILK FRIED CHICKEN ♦ WILD RICE WAFFLE, HONEY-PINK PEPPERCORN SAUCE	131
HERB ROASTED TURKEY	133
DUCK ♦ DIRTY WILD RICE, PECANS, BOURBON	134
GRILLED LAMB PORTERHOUSE CHOPS ♦ MUSTARD BARBECUE SAUCE, CORN AND COLLARD GREEN TART	137
GRILLED VEAL PORTERHOUSE CHOP ♦ FIG CABERNET VINEGAR GLAZE	141
LAMB SAUSAGE ♦ WHITE BEANS, RED ZINFANDEL	143
RACK OF PORK ♦ MOLASSES-MUSTARD GLAZE, SOUR MASH, APPLE BUTTER	144
PAN-ROASTED PORK TENDERLOIN ♦ GREEN TOMATO–PEACH RELISH, GREEN PEA COUSCOUS	147
COUNTRY-STYLE RIBS ♦ BOURBON BARBECUE SAUCE, TOMATO CORN BREAD	149
BROILED HANGER STEAK ♦ HOMEMADE STEAK SAUCE	150
BLACKENED ROASTED PRIME RIB ♦ BÉARNAISE BUTTER	152
PHILADELPHIA-STYLE STRIP STEAK	154
PAN-ROASTED VENISON ♦ RED CABBAGE BREAD PUDDING, CONCORD GRAPE SAUCE	157
GRILLED VENISON CHOPS ♦ BLACKBERRY-SAGE BROWN BUTTER	159

CHICKEN CUTLET
AMERICAN TRIPLE CREAM CHEESE, SOUTHERN HAM, ARUGULA

Here is that American favorite, Chicken Cordon Bleu, deconstructed. This gorgeous dish pulls the soggy ham and cheese out of the stuffing, layering them instead over a crisp, juicy chicken cutlet. The rich triple cream cheese begins to melt when it hits the panko-crusted chicken, which then anchors the paper-thin slices of cured ham to them both. Baby arugula is tossed in a bright, acidic vinaigrette of Dijon mustard and red wine vinegar before being placed atop the dish. The peppery arugula and mustardy vinaigrette cut through the richness of the cheese and complement the salty ham. I serve this at lunch, but it would be wonderful at dinner as well.

Serves 4

Chicken
1 cup all-purpose flour
3 large eggs, lightly beaten
2 cups panko bread crumbs
Kosher salt and freshly ground black pepper
4 (6-ounce) boneless, skinless chicken
    breast halves
6 tablespoons (¾ stick) unsalted butter
2 tablespoons olive oil
¼ pound Red Hawk triple cream cheese, Brie,
    or Camembert, thinly sliced
8 thin slices country ham or prosciutto

Arugula Salad
2 tablespoons red wine vinegar
1 teaspoon Dijon mustard
Kosher salt and freshly ground black pepper
¼ cup extra virgin olive oil
¼ pound baby arugula

1. To cook the chicken, put the flour, eggs, and bread crumbs in 3 separate shallow bowls and season each with salt and pepper.

2. Place each chicken breast between 2 pieces of wax paper and pound to ¼-inch thickness.

3. Season the chicken on both sides with salt and pepper and then dredge each breast in the flour and tap off the excess. Dip into the egg wash and let the excess drip off, then dredge on both sides in the bread crumbs. Place on a wire rack set over a baking sheet.

4. Preheat 2 large nonstick sauté pans over high heat. Add 3 tablespoons of the butter and 1 tablespoon of the oil to each pan and heat until the butter is melted and sizzling. Place 2 breasts in each pan and cook until golden brown, about 4 minutes. Flip the breasts over and continue cooking until golden brown and the chicken is cooked through, about 3 minutes.

5. To make the arugula salad, whisk together the vinegar and mustard in a large bowl. Season with salt and pepper. Slowly whisk in the oil until emulsified. Add the arugula and toss to coat the leaves with the vinaigrette.

6. Transfer each breast to a large plate and immediately top with a few slices of cheese, then a few slices of ham, and some of the arugula salad.

SMOKED CHICKEN
HATCH GREEN CHILE SPOONBREAD, BLACK PEPPER VINEGAR SAUCE

This black pepper vinegar sauce is very much an ode to the vinegar-based barbecue sauce served in the restaurants and homes of eastern North Carolina. When you hear barbecue referred to as "Carolina style," you know it means that your pulled pork, ribs, or chicken will be paired with a tangy, often mustard-laced, and always tomato-free vinegary sauce. If you have the wherewithal—and the will—to cold-smoke your chicken as we do in the restaurant, by all means do so, but simply roasting the chicken in the oven will more than suffice. Either way, you'll be looking at an incredibly flavorful chicken dish.

Serves 4

Black Pepper Vinegar Sauce
¼ cup plus 2 tablespoons Dijon mustard

3 tablespoons honey

¼ cup rice wine vinegar

2 teaspoons freshly ground black pepper

1½ teaspoons kosher salt

⅓ cup canola oil

⅓ cup extra virgin olive oil

Chicken
1 (4-pound) whole chicken, excess fat trimmed, rinsed and patted dry

2 tablespoons canola oil

Kosher salt and freshly ground black pepper

Green Chile Spoonbread (page 185)

1. To make the sauce, whisk together the mustard, honey, vinegar, pepper, and salt in a medium bowl. Combine the canola and olive oils and then slowly add to the mustard mixture, whisking until emulsified. Let sit at room temperature while you prepare the chicken, or cover and refrigerate for up to 2 days. Bring to room temperature before serving.

2. Brush the entire chicken with the oil and lightly season inside and out with salt and pepper. If desired, cold-smoke the chicken for 20 minutes according to the directions on page 249.

3. Preheat the oven to 450°F.

4. Put the chicken, breast side up, on a rack set inside a large roasting pan. Roast the chicken until it begins to turn light golden brown, about 20 minutes. Reduce the heat to 350°F and continue roasting until an instant-read thermometer inserted in the thickest part of the thigh reads 155°F, about 1 hour. Remove the chicken from the oven, tent with foil, and let rest for 15 minutes before carving.

5. Drizzle some of the sauce onto a large platter, top with the carved chicken, and place the spoonbread on the side. Serve extra sauce on the side.

SMOKED CHICKEN POT PIE
SWEET POTATO CRUST

One of my goals with the cuisine at Bar Americain is
to re-create the classics of French brasserie cuisine with
the best of America's ingredients. The other is to put my
spin on those dishes that make up this country's culinary
heritage. This dish is a perfect example of the latter.
Chicken pot pie . . . could it get any more authentically
American than that? It's warm, comforting, and, in this
case, super flavorful and beautiful to boot. I opt for
a flaky, golden-orange sweet potato biscuit crust that
opens up to reveal a garlic- and onion-scented cream
sauce studded with juicy chicken, tender vegetables, and
flecks of parsley. We make this dish with smoked and
roasted chicken at the restaurant, and I love the extra
layer of flavor that cold-smoking adds. If you are up to it,
follow the directions on page 249 and skip the chipotle
in adobo puree or smoked paprika, which approximate
that smokiness in the recipe.

Serves 6 to 8

Sweet Potato Crust
1 large sweet potato
3¾ cups all-purpose flour, plus more for shaping
1½ teaspoons kosher salt
½ teaspoon freshly ground black pepper
½ pound (2 sticks) unsalted butter, cut into
    pieces, chilled
1 large egg
½ cup whole milk
2 large eggs, beaten with 3 tablespoons
    cold water

Pot Pie Filling
4 tablespoons (½ stick) unsalted butter
1 medium Spanish onion, finely diced
3 cloves garlic, finely chopped
¼ cup all-purpose flour
1 quart whole milk, heated, or more if needed
¾ pound cremini mushrooms, quartered and
    sautéed in canola oil until golden brown
2 turnips, peeled, cut into medium dice, blanched
    (see page 249), and drained
2 carrots, cut into matchsticks, blanched
    (see page 249), and drained
1 cup frozen pearl onions, preferably half red
    and half white, blanched (see page 249),
    and drained
1 cup frozen peas, blanched (see page 249)
    and drained
1 (3-pound) roasted chicken, shredded
2 teaspoons pureed canned chipotle chile in
    adobo or 2 teaspoons smoked sweet
    Spanish paprika
Kosher salt and freshly ground black pepper
¼ cup coarsely chopped fresh flat-leaf parsley

1. To make the sweet potato crust, preheat the oven
to 375°F.

2. Prick the sweet potato several times with a fork,
place on a baking sheet, and roast in the oven until
soft, about 45 minutes. Remove from the oven and
let cool slightly. When cool enough to handle, halve
the potato lengthwise and, using a small spoon,
scrape the flesh into a medium bowl; discard the
skin. While the potato is still hot, mash with a potato
masher or fork until slightly smooth. Measure out
1 cup potato.

3. Stir together the flour, salt, and pepper in a large bowl. Cut in the butter until the butter pieces are the size of small peas. Stir together the egg, milk, and sweet potato in a bowl, add the mixture to the flour, and gently mix with a rubber spatula until just combined. Transfer to a lightly floured surface and lightly knead the dough until it just comes together. Form into a circle and flatten slightly. Wrap in plastic wrap and refrigerate until chilled, at least 1 hour or overnight.

4. Meanwhile, make the filling. Melt the butter in a medium saucepan over high heat. Add the diced onion and cook until soft, about 4 minutes. Add the garlic and cook for 1 minute. Add the flour and cook, stirring occasionally, until deep golden brown, about 3 minutes. Slowly whisk in the hot milk and cook until thickened, 5 minutes. Reduce the heat to medium and cook, whisking occasionally, for 5 minutes. If the mixture is too thick to pour easily, thin it with a little extra milk.

5. Add the mushrooms, turnips, carrots, pearl onions, peas, chicken, and chipotle puree to the sauce and fold gently to combine. Season the sauce with salt and pepper and stir in the parsley. The filling can be made a day in advance, covered, and refrigerated.

6. Preheat the oven to 375°F.

7. For individual servings, divide the dough in half and roll each half out on a lightly floured surface until ⅛ inch thick. Invert individual ovenproof bowls onto the rolled crust and, using a sharp knife, cut circles around the outside of the bowls that are slightly larger than each bowl. Fill the bowls three-quarters of the way with the chicken mixture, making sure each serving has a nice amount of chicken, vegetables, and sauce. Carefully cap each crock with a pastry round, pressing the dough around the rim to form a seal. Brush the tops with the egg wash and season with salt and pepper. Make a small slit in the center of each using a paring knife. Alternatively, roll one large crust and use it to top a family-style pot pie in a 10-inch baking dish.

8. Transfer the pies to baking sheets and bake until the crust is golden brown and the filling is bubbly, 15 to 18 minutes for individual pot pies and 25 to 30 minutes for one large pot pie. Remove from the oven and let sit for 5 minutes before serving.

BUTTERMILK FRIED CHICKEN
WILD RICE WAFFLE, HONEY–PINK PEPPERCORN SAUCE

This dish is brought to you straight from Harlem. Fried chicken and waffles was invented by the singers and musicians who performed in Harlem's storied jazz age. Those gigs would last until the early hours of the morning, when the musicians spilled out into the neighborhood's restaurants. Hungry after a long night and still in their evening clothes and mind-sets, they found fried chicken fit the bill. At the same time, the sun would be rising, and a breakfast of waffles sounded pretty good, too. And so waffles became a bed for fried chicken, and a soul-food classic was born. I put my own riff on the dish by adding nutty wild rice to the waffles and serving the whole thing up with a sauce of honey and sweet, mildly peppery pink peppercorns.

Serves 6 to 8

Chicken
6 cups buttermilk

Kosher salt

2 teaspoons ground chile de árbol or
  2 tablespoons hot sauce

2 (3- to 4-pound) chickens, each cut
  into 8 pieces

4 cups all-purpose flour

1 tablespoon garlic powder

1 tablespoon onion powder

1 tablespoon smoked sweet Spanish paprika

2 teaspoons cayenne

Freshly ground black pepper

Canola or peanut oil, for deep-frying

Honey–Pink Peppercorn Sauce (page 132)

Wild Rice Waffles
1½ cups all-purpose flour

1½ cups whole wheat flour

1½ tablespoons sugar

1 tablespoon plus 1 teaspoon baking powder

2 teaspoons baking soda

1 teaspoon kosher salt

4 cups buttermilk

4 large eggs

½ cup canola oil

¾ cup overcooked wild rice

Unsalted butter, melted, for the waffle maker

1. To cook the chicken, whisk together 4 cups of the buttermilk, 2 tablespoons salt, and the chile de árbol in a large bowl or baking dish. Add the chicken, turn to coat, cover, and refrigerate for at least 4 hours or overnight.

2. Pour the remaining 2 cups buttermilk into a bowl. Stir together the flour, garlic and onion powders, paprika, and cayenne in a large bowl, season generously with salt and pepper, and then divide between 2 shallow platters. Drain the chicken in a colander and pat it dry. Dredge the pieces a few at a time in one platter of the flour mixture, pat off any excess, then dip in the buttermilk and allow any excess to drain off. Dredge in the second platter of flour and pat off the excess. Put the chicken pieces on a wire rack set over a baking sheet.

3. Pour about 3 inches of oil into a deep cast-iron skillet; the oil should not come more than halfway up the sides of the pan. Put the skillet over medium-high heat and heat the oil to 375°F on a deep-fat thermometer. Add the chicken to the hot oil, 3 or 4 pieces at a time, and fry, turning the pieces occasionally, until evenly golden brown and cooked through, about 20 minutes. Remove from the oil with a slotted spoon and transfer to a rack to drain; repeat to cook the remaining pieces.

(recipe continues)

4. To make the waffles, whisk together the flours, sugar, baking powder, baking soda, and salt in a large bowl.

5. Whisk together the buttermilk, eggs, and oil in a separate large bowl. Pour over the flour mixture and whisk until the mixture just comes together. Add the wild rice and fold until just combined. Let rest for 10 minutes.

6. While the mixture is resting, heat the waffle maker. Brush the waffle grates with some melted butter and cook the waffles according to the manufacturer's directions.

7. Serve the fried chicken with waffles and drizzle both with some of the honey–pink peppercorn sauce.

HONEY–PINK PEPPERCORN SAUCE
Makes 1 cup

1 cup honey
2 teaspoons pink peppercorns, toasted
   (see page 250) and coarsely chopped
Grated zest of 1 lime
Juice of 2 limes
Kosher salt and freshly ground black pepper

Stir together the honey, peppercorns, lime zest, and juice in a small bowl and season with salt and pepper. Cover and let sit at room temperature for at least 30 minutes or refrigerate for up to 1 day. Bring to room temperature before serving.

HERB ROASTED TURKEY

Thanksgiving is hands-down my favorite holiday. Bar Americain is open each year for Thanksgiving, and we typically serve about six hundred people before the day is over. No matter how many wonderful selections we offer on the abbreviated holiday menu, without fail turkey is the biggest seller—partly because people love it and partly, I think, out of a sense of tradition. This is the turkey that I serve at Bar Americain, with only the dressing and sides changing from year to year. This year I am pairing the all-American bird with all-American ingredients: wild mushrooms and Pinot Noir from the Pacific Northwest, figs from California, cranberries from Maine, bacon from Kentucky, and sweet potatoes from Georgia.

Serves 8

1 (17-pound) turkey, rinsed well and patted dry
10 tablespoons (1¼ sticks) unsalted butter, softened
2 tablespoons finely chopped fresh flat-leaf parsley
1 tablespoon finely chopped fresh sage
1 tablespoon finely chopped fresh rosemary
1 tablespoon finely chopped fresh thyme
Kosher salt and freshly ground black pepper
6 cups chicken stock, homemade (page 240) or store-bought
3 large carrots, cut into 1-inch pieces
3 large stalks celery, cut into 1-inch pieces
2 large onions, quartered

1. Remove the turkey from the refrigerator 1 hour before roasting.

2. Combine the butter, parsley, sage, rosemary, and thyme in a food processor and process until smooth. Season with salt and pepper.

3. Preheat the oven to 450°F.

4. Put 4 cups of the chicken stock in a medium saucepan and keep warm over low heat.

5. Season the cavity of the turkey with salt and pepper and fill the cavity with half of the carrots, celery, and onions. Rub the entire turkey with the herb butter and season liberally with salt and pepper.

6. Scatter the remaining vegetables on the bottom of a large roasting pan. Fit a rack over the vegetables and put the turkey on top of the rack. Pour the remaining 2 cups stock into the bottom of the roasting pan and carefully put the pan in the oven. Roast until the turkey is light golden brown, about 45 minutes.

7. Reduce the oven temperature to 350°F and continue roasting, basting with the warm chicken stock every 15 minutes, until an instant-read thermometer inserted in the thigh registers 160°F, about 2½ hours longer.

8. Remove the turkey from the oven, transfer to a large cutting board, and tent loosely with foil. Let rest for 30 minutes before carving.

9. Strain the stock in the bottom of the roasting pan through a strainer lined with cheesecloth or paper towels into a medium saucepan. Discard the solids. Boil the stock until reduced to a sauce consistency (see page 250). Arrange the turkey on a large platter and drizzle with the reduced stock.

DUCK
DIRTY WILD RICE, PECANS, BOURBON

Dirty rice is a traditional Cajun dish of white rice cooked with chopped chicken livers. The liver darkens, or "dirties," the rice and infuses it with its mild yet distinctive taste. My version is classically flavored but prepared in a not-so-traditional manner: I use Arborio rice, cook it as I would a risotto, and fold in cooked wild rice as one of the last steps so that its nutty flavor and chewy crunch run throughout the dish. I think of this as a Louisiana-style dish, and the southern flavors of deep bourbon and sweet, crunchy pecans are fitting accomplices to the rich duck and aromatic rice.

Serves 4

Dirty Rice
1 quart chicken stock, homemade (page 240) or store-bought
4 tablespoons canola oil
½ pound chicken livers
Kosher salt and freshly ground black pepper
1 tablespoon unsalted butter
1 stalk celery, finely diced
2 cloves garlic, finely chopped
2 jalapeño chiles, finely diced
1 yellow bell pepper, roasted, peeled, seeded, and finely diced (see page 250)
1 red bell pepper, roasted, peeled, seeded, and finely diced (see page 250)
1 cup Arborio rice
1 cup cooked wild rice
2 tablespoons chopped fresh flat-leaf parsley
2 teaspoons chopped fresh thyme
2 tablespoons pure maple syrup
¼ cup pecans, toasted (see page 250) and chopped

Pan-Roasted Duck
4 (8-ounce) Muscovy duck breasts, extra fat trimmed off
Kosher salt and freshly ground black pepper
Bourbon Sauce (page 136)

1. Preheat the oven to 375°F.

2. To cook the rice, heat the stock in a medium saucepan and then keep warm over low heat.

3. Heat 2 tablespoons of the oil in a large sauté pan over high heat until the oil begins to shimmer. Pat the chicken livers dry with paper towels and season with salt and pepper. Cook, turning once, until golden brown and cooked to medium, about 5 minutes. Remove from the heat, let cool slightly, and then coarsely chop. Set aside.

4. To cook the duck, heat a large ovenproof sauté pan over medium heat. Score the skin of the duck breasts with a sharp knife, cutting ⅛ inch into the skin at 1-inch intervals in a crosshatch pattern. Season both sides of the duck with salt and pepper. Place the breasts in the pan, skin side down, and cook until golden brown and the fat has rendered, about 10 minutes. Carefully drain most of the fat from the pan, turn the breasts over, and roast in the oven to medium-rare, about 10 minutes longer. Remove from the oven, tent loosely with foil, and let rest for 10 minutes before slicing.

5. While the duck is cooking, heat the remaining 2 tablespoons oil and the butter in a large deep sauté pan over medium heat. Add the celery, garlic, and jalapeños and cook until soft, 4 minutes. Add the roasted yellow and red peppers and cook for 1 minute. Add the Arborio rice, stir to coat, and cook for 1 minute.

6. Begin adding the hot stock ½ cup at a time to the rice, stirring constantly until absorbed. Continue adding stock and stirring until the rice is al dente, about 20 minutes. You may not need all of the stock.

7. Stir in the wild rice, chicken livers, parsley, thyme, and maple syrup and heat through, 1 to 2 minutes. Transfer to a large bowl or platter and top with the toasted pecans.

8. Slice the duck crosswise into ½-inch-thick slices, transfer to a platter, and drizzle with the bourbon sauce. Serve extra sauce on the side.

(recipe continues)

BOURBON SAUCE
Makes about 1½ cups

2 tablespoons canola oil

1 tablespoon unsalted butter plus 2 tablespoons,
   chilled, cut into pieces

1 large carrot, diced

1 medium onion, diced

1 stalk celery, diced

1 leek, white and light green parts, sliced and
   rinsed well

Kosher salt and freshly ground black pepper

1 cup plus 2 tablespoons bourbon

1 quart chicken stock, homemade (page 240)
   or store-bought

4 sprigs fresh thyme, plus 2 teaspoons finely
   chopped for garnish

1. Heat the oil and 1 tablespoon butter in a medium saucepan over medium heat. Add the carrot, onion, celery, and leek, season with salt and pepper, and cook until soft, stirring occasionally, about 7 minutes.

2. Increase the heat to high, add 1 cup of the bourbon, and boil until completely evaporated, about 5 minutes. Add the stock and thyme sprigs and boil until reduced to a sauce consistency (see page 250), about 1½ cups, 20 minutes.

3. Strain the sauce through a fine-mesh strainer into a bowl and return to the saucepan. Stir in the 2 tablespoons chilled butter, the remaining 2 table-spoons bourbon, and the chopped thyme. Season the sauce with salt and pepper to taste and keep warm.

GRILLED LAMB PORTERHOUSE CHOPS
MUSTARD BARBECUE SAUCE, CORN AND COLLARD GREEN TART

Many people think the term *porterhouse* refers to the size of the steak, but that is not the case. Porterhouse is an on-the-bone cut with a portion of the flavorful strip on one side of the bone and the tender filet on the other. With its lacquering of barbecue sauce and side of a corn-collard green tart, this dish is an ode to the South. The Carolinas are fanatical about mustard-based barbecue sauces. Mustard lends a tangy heat that is offset by dark, sweet molasses, and both are mellowed by mild honey and light rice wine vinegar. This barbecue sauce is as at home with lamb as it is with the smoked pork of the Carolinas. The tart's savory filling is basically a corn pudding run through with strips of collard greens.

Serves 4

Corn and Collard Green Tart
1¼ cups all-purpose flour, plus more for rolling
½ teaspoon kosher salt
8 tablespoons (1 stick) unsalted butter, cut into pieces, chilled
4 to 6 tablespoons ice water
2 tablespoons canola oil
¾ cup fresh or frozen corn kernels
Kosher salt and freshly ground black pepper
3 large eggs
3 tablespoons cream cheese, at room temperature
1 cup heavy cream
½ recipe Smoked Chile Collard Greens (page 174), drained on paper towels and cooled

Lamb Porterhouse Chops
½ cup Dijon mustard
¼ cup ketchup
¼ cup molasses
¼ cup honey
2 tablespoons pure maple syrup
2 tablespoons rice wine vinegar
Kosher salt and freshly ground black pepper
4 (6- to 7-ounce) lamb porterhouse chops
Parsley Oil (page 239; optional), for garnish

1. To make the tart, combine the flour and salt in a food processor and pulse a few times to combine. Scatter the butter over the top of the flour and pulse until the mixture resembles coarse meal, 6 to 8 pulses.

2. With the machine running, add 4 tablespoons ice water in a slow, steady stream through the feed tube. Pulse until the dough holds together without being wet or sticky. To test, squeeze a small amount together: If it holds together, it is ready. If it is crumbly, add up to 2 tablespoons more ice water, 1 tablespoon at a time. Form the dough into a flat disk, cover with plastic wrap, and refrigerate until cold, at least 1 hour and up to 24 hours.

3. Roll out the dough to a 12-inch round on a floured surface. Transfer to a 9-inch tart pan with a removable bottom. Trim the dough overhang to 1 inch. Fold the overhang in and press, forming a double-thick high-standing side. Pierce the crust all over with a fork. Freeze the crust for 30 minutes and up to 1 month.

4. Position a rack in center of oven and preheat the oven to 400°F.

5. Bake the crust on a baking sheet, piercing with a fork if the crust bubbles in places, until light golden brown, about 20 minutes. Remove from the oven, keeping the crust on the baking sheet, and let cool slightly. Reduce the oven temperature to 350°F.

(recipe continues)

6. Heat the oil in a medium sauté pan over high heat. Add the corn, season with salt and pepper, and cook until the corn is light golden brown and tender, about 5 minutes. Let cool slightly.

7 Whisk together the eggs and cream cheese in a medium bowl until smooth. Whisk in the cream, corn, and collard greens and season with salt and pepper. Pour into the prepared tart shell and bake until the sides of the filling are slightly puffed and the center still jiggles slightly, about 40 minutes. Remove the tart from the oven and let cool at room temperature for at least 15 minutes before serving. The tart can be served hot or at room temperature.

8. To make the barbecue sauce for the lamb chops, whisk together the mustard, ketchup, molasses, honey, maple syrup, and vinegar in a small bowl and season with salt and pepper. Cover and let sit at room temperature for at least 30 minutes or refrigerate for up to 2 days. Bring to room temperature before serving.

9. Preheat the grill to high or heat a grill pan over high heat. Pour half of the barbecue sauce into a serving bowl and set aside. Season the lamb on both sides with salt and pepper and brush liberally with some of the rest of the sauce. Place the chops on the grill and cook until golden brown and slightly charred, 3 to 4 minutes. Brush with more of the sauce, turn the chops over, and continue grilling to medium, 2 to 3 minutes more, brushing the top with more of the sauce. Remove the chops from the grill, brush with some of the reserved sauce, and let rest for 5 minutes.

10. Serve 1 chop per person with a slice of corn and collard green tart and the reserved sauce on the side. Garnish with parsley oil if desired.

GRILLED VEAL PORTERHOUSE CHOP
FIG CABERNET VINEGAR GLAZE

Tender veal is most commonly served in lighter preparations because of its delicate nature, but the porterhouse cut is substantial enough to allow for a truly rich and deeply flavorful sauce such as this one. Intensely sweet dried figs steeped in wine join a reduction of wine and veal stock to form a syrupy glaze that coats the veal in flavor. Cabernet vinegar (though another red wine vinegar will do) balances the figs' inherent sweetness with its bright acidity. Uncommon as they are, veal porterhouse chops make this a memorable, special-occasion dish, but you could certainly substitute thick-cut pork chops with excellent results.

Serves 4

Fig Cabernet Glaze

2 cups Cabernet Sauvignon

8 dried figs, halved

1 quart store-bought veal stock (see Sources) or chicken stock, homemade (page 240) or store-bought

2 shallots, finely diced

2 tablespoons Cabernet vinegar or other red wine vinegar

1 tablespoon honey

Kosher salt and freshly ground black pepper

Grilled Veal Porterhouse Chops

4 (14-ounce) veal porterhouse chops, trimmed of excess fat

2 tablespoons canola oil

Kosher salt and freshly ground black pepper

Fresh flat-leaf parsley sprigs, for garnish

1. To make the glaze, bring 1 cup of the wine to a simmer in a small saucepan. Remove from the heat, add the figs, and let steep while you prepare the glaze.

2. Put the veal stock in a medium saucepan and bring to a boil over high heat. Cook until reduced by half to 2 cups, about 15 minutes. Add the shallots and remaining 1 cup wine to the stock and continue cooking over high heat, stirring occasionally, until reduced to a sauce consistency (see page 250), about 25 minutes. Stir in the vinegar and honey and season with salt and pepper. Drain the figs and stir into the sauce. Keep warm. The glaze can be made 1 day in advance and stored covered in the refrigerator. Reheat before serving.

3. Remove the chops from the refrigerator 20 minutes before grilling. Preheat the grill to high or heat a grill pan over high heat.

4. Brush both sides of the chops with the oil and season with salt and pepper. Put the chops on the grill or in the grill pan and cook until golden brown and slightly charred, about 5 minutes. Turn the chops over, reduce the heat to medium, and continue cooking until the bottoms are golden brown and slightly charred and the chops are cooked to 140°F internal temperature on a meat thermometer, about 8 minutes longer. Remove the chops from the heat and let rest for 5 minutes.

5. Place the chops on 4 large dinner plates. Ladle some of the glaze over each chop and garnish with parsley sprigs.

LAMB SAUSAGE
WHITE BEANS, RED ZINFANDEL

I always tell people that I want Bar Americain to feel French but taste American. This is a classic bistro or brasserie dish that you would find in Europe, and by making it my own, perhaps with a California Zinfandel wine and vinegar, I think we manage to do just that—feel French, taste American. This is an incredibly comforting dish capable of warming your whole being on a cold fall or winter's day. I like the spicy heat of merguez sausage in this dish, but you could certainly use another variety of lamb or even pork sausage if you so choose.

Serves 4

½ pound (1½ cups) dried white beans, such as Great Northern or cannellini, or 2 (15½-ounce) cans white beans
Kosher salt and freshly ground black pepper
8 links merguez sausage (about 1 pound)
4 tablespoons canola oil
3 shallots, finely diced
2 cloves garlic, finely chopped
2 red bell peppers, roasted, peeled, seeded, and diced (see page 250)
¼ cup Zinfandel vinegar or other red wine vinegar
¼ cup extra virgin olive oil
¼ cup plus 1 tablespoon chopped fresh flat-leaf parsley
3 tablespoons chopped fresh mint leaves
2 teaspoons honey
Zinfandel Glaze (recipe follows)

1. If using dried beans, cover them by at least 2 inches with cold water and let soak for at least 8 hours or overnight. Drain the beans, put them in a medium pot, and cover by 2 inches with cold water. Bring to a boil over high heat. Add 1 tablespoon salt, lower the heat to medium, cover the pot, and cook until tender, about 1 hour. Drain well if needed.

2. If using canned beans, drain them, rinse well in cold water, and drain again.

3. Heat a grill pan or sauté pan over high heat. Brush the sausage with 2 tablespoons of the canola oil and grill or sauté until golden brown on both sides and just cooked through, about 3 minutes per side. Transfer to a plate lined with paper towels.

4. Heat the remaining 2 tablespoons canola oil in a large sauté pan over medium heat, add the shallots and garlic, and cook until soft, about 3 minutes. Add the red pepper and cook for 1 minute.

5. Put the beans in a large bowl and add the shallot mixture, vinegar, olive oil, ¼ cup of the parsley, 2 tablespoons of the mint, and the honey. Season with salt and pepper and stir gently to combine.

6. Divide the beans among 4 large dinner plates and top with the sausages. Drizzle with some of the Zinfandel glaze and garnish with the remaining 1 tablespoon chopped parsley and 1 tablespoon chopped mint.

ZINFANDEL GLAZE
Makes about ¾ cup

1 (750-ml) bottle red Zinfandel
2 tablespoons honey
2 tablespoons canola oil
Kosher salt and freshly ground black pepper

1. Put the wine in a medium nonreactive saucepan over high heat, bring to a boil, and cook, stirring occasionally, until thickened and reduced to about ½ cup, about 30 minutes.

2. Remove from the heat, stir in the honey, and let cool slightly. Whisk in the oil and season with salt and pepper. Keep warm.

APPLE BUTTER
Makes about 1½ cups

2 tablespoons canola oil
½ small Spanish onion, finely chopped
1 clove garlic, finely chopped
2 large Granny Smith apples, peeled, cored,
    and chopped
3 tablespoons light brown sugar
1 teaspoon ground cinnamon
¼ teaspoon kosher salt
½ pound (2 sticks) unsalted butter, softened

1. Heat the oil in a large sauté pan over medium heat. Add the onion and garlic and cook until soft, 3 to 4 minutes. Add the apples, brown sugar, and ¼ cup water and cook until the apples are very soft, 10 minutes. Stir in the cinnamon and salt and cook for 1 minute. Remove the mixture from the heat and let cool.

2. Transfer the mixture to a food processor along with the butter and process until slightly chunky. Scrape into a small bowl, cover, and refrigerate for at least 1 hour and up to 24 hours to allow the flavors to meld. Bring to room temperature before serving.

PAN-ROASTED PORK TENDERLOIN
GREEN TOMATO-PEACH RELISH, GREEN PEA COUSCOUS

Ray Charles must have been in my head when I designed this dish, because it's all about Georgia. The green tomato-peach relish is a natural, and not only because both ingredients are beloved by Georgians. The tartness of the green tomatoes is evenly matched by the honey sweetness of the peaches, and the resulting relish is fresh, incredibly flavorful, and totally balanced. Pork tenderloin is lean, has very little fat, and cooks quickly, so your kitchen stays cool while you eat well. This really is a wonderful summer dish.

Serves 4 to 6

4 tablespoons canola oil

2 pounds pork tenderloin

Kosher salt and freshly ground black pepper

1 small Spanish onion, finely diced

2 cloves garlic, finely chopped

4 tablespoons fresh lime juice

¼ cup plus 2 tablespoons white wine vinegar

1 large green tomato, halved, seeded, and finely diced

2 ripe peaches, peeled, halved, pitted, and finely diced

2 tablespoons sugar

¼ cup chopped fresh flat-leaf parsley

2 green onions, green and pale green parts, thinly sliced

2 teaspoons honey

Green Pea Couscous (page 168)

1. Preheat the oven to 400°F.

2. Heat 2 tablespoons of the oil in a medium oven-proof sauté pan over high heat until the oil begins to shimmer. Season the tenderloin on both sides with salt and pepper. Place the pork in the pan and sear on all sides until golden brown, about 8 minutes.

3. Transfer the pan to the oven and roast the pork to medium (an internal temperature of 150°F), about 10 minutes. Remove from the oven, tent loosely with foil, and let rest for 10 minutes before slicing ½ inch thick.

4. While the pork is roasting, heat the remaining 2 tablespoons oil in a large sauté pan over high heat. Add the onion and cook until soft, about 4 minutes. Add the garlic and cook for 30 seconds. Stir in 2 tablespoons of the lime juice and ¼ cup of the vinegar and boil until reduced, 8 to 10 minutes.

5. Add the tomato, peaches, and sugar, reduce the heat to medium, and cook slowly until the mixture is slightly soft but the peaches retain some of their shape, 8 to 10 minutes. Remove from the heat, stir in the remaining 2 tablespoons vinegar and 2 tablespoons lime juice, the parsley, green onions, and honey. Season with salt and pepper. Scrape the relish into a bowl and let cool to room temperature before serving.

6. Serve slices of the pork on a bed of couscous and top with the relish.

COUNTRY-STYLE RIBS
BOURBON BARBECUE SAUCE, TOMATO CORN BREAD

This is barbecue belt cooking all the way. I don't care if you're in Austin, Texas, or Manhattan, New York—if ribs are on the menu, you've got to roll up your shirt sleeves and have a big stack of napkins ready. This dish has New Yorkers doing just that when it makes its weekly appearance at Bar Americain. Racks of meaty ribs are dressed up with a smoky spice rub for extra flavor. The rich barbecue sauce, spiked with the molasseslike flavor of bourbon, will leave even the most refined diners licking their fingers. It wouldn't be proper barbecue without some corn bread to mop up every last delicious bit of flavor from the plate, and I like to serve this dish with a savory tomato one.

Serves 4

4 cups hickory or oak wood chips

¼ cup ground ancho chile

2 tablespoons smoked sweet Spanish paprika

2 tablespoons freshly ground black pepper

2 tablespoons dry mustard

2 tablespoons kosher salt

2 tablespoons ground coriander

1 tablespoon dried oregano

1 tablespoon ground cumin

2 teaspoons ground chile de árbol

2 racks country pork ribs (12 ribs each), membrane removed

¼ cup canola oil

Bourbon Barbecue Sauce (page 236)

Tomato Corn Bread (page 191)

1. Soak the wood chips in water for at least 30 minutes. Drain well.

2. Stir together the ground ancho, paprika, black pepper, dry mustard, salt, coriander, oregano, cumin, and ground chile de árbol in a small bowl.

3. Brush both sides of the racks with the oil and rub liberally with the spice mixture. Wrap in plastic and refrigerate for at least 12 hours and up to 24 hours. Remove the ribs from the refrigerator 45 minutes before smoking to allow them to come to room temperature.

4. Stuff several sheets of newspaper in the bottom of a charcoal chimney starter. Fill the chimney to the top with charcoal. Remove the top rack from your grill. Place the chimney on the lower rack. Light the newspaper and let the charcoal burn until the coals are gray on the outside, about 20 minutes.

5. Open the bottom vent on the grill. Turn out the hot charcoal onto one side of the bottom rack. Using a metal spatula, spread the charcoal to cover approximately one-third of the rack and then scatter half of the soaked wood chips over the charcoal.

6. Return the top rack to the grill. Place an oven thermometer to one side of the rack to allow you to monitor the temperature of the grill, which should stay between 250°F and 300°F at all times. (Check the temperature every 10 minutes.)

7. Place the ribs on the rack to the side of the coals, not directly over them, and cover the grill. Pour one-quarter of the bourbon barbecue sauce into a separate container and set aside. Cook, turning the ribs and basting them with the rest of the barbecue sauce every 20 minutes, until the meat is very tender when pierced with a knife, about 1½ hours. After the first 30 minutes of cooking, light additional charcoal as before, placing the chimney starter on a heat-proof surface. When the temperature in the grill drops below 250°F, use oven mitts to lift off the top rack with the ribs in place and set on a heatproof surface. Using tongs, add hot charcoal from the chimney starter to the bottom rack and then scatter the remaining wood chips on top. Return the rack of ribs and cover the grill with the lid.

8. Transfer the ribs to a baking sheet; brush with the reserved barbecue sauce and let stand for 10 minutes. Cut the meat between the bones to separate the ribs and serve with the tomato corn bread.

BROILED HANGER STEAK
HOMEMADE STEAK SAUCE

A favorite cut of butchers, hanger steak is also the steak of choice for the quintessential French bistro dish steak frites. It may not have the cachet of a hulking porterhouse or a pricey filet, but what it lacks in name it more than makes up for in taste. Hanger steak has a rich, beefy flavor that is enhanced here by a savory rub. Bar Americain's steak sauce is a balanced blend of the sweet and sharp notes of molasses, honey, Dijon mustard, and horseradish. You could serve this steak with Fries Americain (page 164) for your own steak frites, or you could make it the centerpiece of an American steakhouse meal by pairing it with Brooklyn Hash Browns (page 163) and Creamed Kale (page 169). (Both the rub and the steak sauce are available for purchase at bobbyflay.com.)

Serves 4

Steak Sauce
¼ cup Dijon mustard
¼ cup whole grain mustard
½ cup molasses
3 tablespoons prepared horseradish, drained
2 tablespoons honey
2 tablespoons ketchup
Kosher salt and freshly ground black pepper

Hanger Steaks
4 (8-ounce) hanger steaks
4 tablespoons (½ stick) unsalted butter, softened
Kosher salt and freshly ground black pepper
Spice Rub (recipe follows)
Parsley Oil (page 239; optional), for garnish

1. To make the sauce, whisk together the mustards, molasses, horseradish, honey, and ketchup and season with salt and pepper. Cover and let sit at room temperature for at least 30 minutes before serving, or cover and refrigerate for up to 2 days and then bring back to room temperature.

2. Remove the steaks from the refrigerator 20 minutes before cooking.

3. Put an oven rack in the upper center of the oven. Preheat the broiler.

4. Pat both sides of the steaks dry with paper towels. Brush both sides of the steaks with the butter and season with salt and pepper. Season one side of each steak with some of the rub mixture. Place the steaks on a wire rack set over a rimmed baking sheet or on a broiler pan, rub side up. Broil the top side of the steaks until golden brown and slightly charred, about 4 minutes. Turn the steaks over and continue broiling until golden brown and cooked to medium-rare, 4 to 5 minutes. Remove from the oven and let rest for 5 minutes before serving.

5. Serve the steaks with the sauce on top or on the side and garnish with parsley oil if desired.

SPICE RUB
Makes ⅓ cup

3 tablespoons smoked sweet Spanish paprika
2 teaspoons ground ancho chile
1 teaspoon ground cumin
1 teaspoon ground coriander
1 teaspoon dry mustard
1 teaspoon dried oregano
¾ teaspoon kosher salt
¾ teaspoon freshly ground black pepper

Mix together the paprika, ground ancho, cumin, coriander, mustard, oregano, salt, and pepper in a small bowl.

BLACKENED ROASTED PRIME RIB
BÉARNAISE BUTTER

Look no further for your next special-occasion meal, because this is it. Also known as a standing rib roast, this cut—tender, juicy, and loaded with flavor—is the king of beef. And as long as we're celebrating, this dish is pushed to its over-the-top status by the accompanying béarnaise butter. This deceptively simple compound butter with shallots, tarragon, and a bit of tangy vinegar delivers the delicately herbal, luscious taste of a rich béarnaise sauce without the hassle and heaviness of its hollandaise base. The only thing I find lacking in most prime rib dishes is that crusty exterior I love, but I've taken care of that by borrowing a technique from my friends in Louisiana—blackening. It encrusts the luscious meat in an extra layer of flavor and texture.

Serves 8

1 (8–pound) prime rib roast (about 4 ribs), trimmed

5 cloves garlic, sliced paper-thin

¾ cup canola oil

2 tablespoons finely chopped fresh thyme

Kosher salt and freshly ground black pepper

½ cup smoked sweet Spanish paprika

2 tablespoons ground ancho chile

2 tablespoons ground pasilla chile

1 tablespoon freshly ground white pepper

1 tablespoon freshly ground black pepper

2 teaspoons dried thyme

2 teaspoons dried oregano

2 teaspoons onion powder

1 teaspoon garlic powder

1 teaspoon celery salt

Béarnaise Butter (recipe follows)

Fresh tarragon leaves, for serving

1. With a sharp paring knife, make a series of ½-inch-deep holes every 2 inches all over the roast. Insert a garlic slice in every hole. Whisk ¼ cup of the oil with the fresh thyme in a small bowl and rub the mixture over the entire roast. Place the roast in a large baking dish, cover with foil, and let marinate in the refrigerator for at least 4 hours and up to 12 hours.

2. Remove the roast from the oven 1 hour before cooking.

3. Preheat the oven to 425°F.

4. Season the roast all over with salt and pepper. Put a rack in a roasting pan and place the roast on the rack. Roast in the oven for 30 minutes. Reduce the oven temperature to 325°F and continue roasting until an instant-read thermometer inserted into the meat registers 135°F for medium-rare, 1 to 1¼ hours longer. Remove the roast from the oven and let rest for 30 minutes.

5. Whisk together the paprika, ground ancho, ground pasilla, white pepper, black pepper, dried thyme, dried oregano, onion powder, garlic powder, and celery salt in a small bowl.

6. Slice the meat 1 inch thick and place on rimmed baking sheets. Rub the top side of each slice with approximately 2 tablespoons of the spice rub.

7. Heat a cast-iron griddle or skillet or a large nonstick sauté pan over high heat until almost smoking. Working in batches, brush the pan liberally with some of the remaining ½ cup oil and sear the steaks, rub side down, until blackened, about 2 minutes.

8. Serve the steaks blackened side up, topped with some of the béarnaise butter and tarragon leaves.

BÉARNAISE BUTTER
Makes about 1¼ cups

½ cup white wine vinegar

2 tablespoons dry white wine

1 large or 2 small shallots, finely diced

½ teaspoon black peppercorns

4 tablespoons finely chopped fresh tarragon

½ pound (2 sticks) unsalted butter, softened

1 teaspoon kosher salt

⅛ teaspoon coarsely ground black pepper

2 tablespoons finely chopped fresh flat-leaf parsley

1. Combine the vinegar, wine, shallot, peppercorns, and 2 tablespoons of the tarragon in a small saucepan. Bring to a boil over high heat and cook until reduced to about 3 tablespoons, about 8 minutes. Strain into a small bowl, pressing against the solids to extract as much liquid as possible. Let the liquid cool to room temperature. Discard the solids.

2. Put the butter into a medium bowl, add the cooled liquid, the remaining 2 tablespoons tarragon, the salt, coarsely ground black pepper, and parsley, and mix to combine. Cover and refrigerate for at least 1 hour and up to 2 days to allow the flavors to meld. Remove from the refrigerator 30 minutes before using.

PHILADELPHIA-STYLE STRIP STEAK

I first brought this steak out at Bobby Flay Steak in Atlantic City. It caused enough of a stir to prompt me to serve it at Bar Americain, where, to the delight of our patrons, it is Saturday's plate of the day. Flavorful, juicy strip steaks are massaged with a chile-laden spice rub and topped with sweet golden caramelized onions—because I definitely order my Philly cheese steak "wit" onions! The cheese choice has always been more of a dilemma for me—the flavor of provolone is far superior to that of classic Cheez Whiz, but I love the smooth, melted texture of the Whiz. I created my own answer to that age-old dilemma for this steak: the provolone sauce is creamy, luscious, and full of sharp cheese flavor. Seriously, this steak is drool-worthy good.

Serves 4

Steaks

4 (12-ounce) boneless strip steaks, trimmed of fat

2 tablespoons canola oil

1½ tablespoons kosher salt

Spice Rub (page 150)

Caramelized Onions (recipe follows)

Steak Sauce (page 150; optional)

Fresh flat-leaf parsley leaves, for garnish

Provolone Sauce

1 tablespoon unsalted butter

1 tablespoon all-purpose flour

2 cups whole milk, plus more if needed, heated

½ pound aged provolone cheese, grated (2 cups)

¼ cup freshly grated Parmesan cheese

1 teaspoon kosher salt

¼ teaspoon freshly ground black pepper

1. To cook the steaks, preheat the broiler.

2. Brush both sides of each steak with the oil and season both sides with the salt. Rub one side of each steak with the spice rub and place the steaks, rub side up, on a broiler pan. Broil until the top of each steak is golden brown and slightly charred, 4 to 6 minutes. Turn the steaks over and continue broiling to medium-rare, 4 to 6 minutes. Remove from the heat and let rest for 5 minutes before serving.

3. To make the cheese sauce, melt the butter in a medium saucepan over medium heat. Whisk in the flour and cook for 1 minute. Slowly whisk in the warm milk and cook, whisking constantly, until thickened, 4 to 5 minutes. If the mixture is too thick to pour easily, thin it with a little extra milk. Remove the mixture from the heat and whisk in the provolone, Parmesan, salt, and pepper.

4. Ladle some of the cheese sauce onto 4 large dinner plates. Place the steaks on top of the sauce, top each steak with some of the caramelized onions, and drizzle with a few tablespoons of steak sauce if desired. Garnish with parsley.

CARAMELIZED ONIONS
Makes about 1 cup

2 tablespoons unsalted butter

1 tablespoon canola oil

3 large Spanish onions, halved and thinly sliced

1 teaspoon kosher salt

¼ teaspoon freshly ground black pepper

Heat the butter and oil in a large sauté pan over medium heat. Add the onions, salt, and pepper and cook slowly, stirring occasionally, until golden brown and caramelized, about 45 minutes. The onions can be made in advance, covered, and refrigerated for up to 2 days. Reheat before serving.

PAN-ROASTED VENISON
RED CABBAGE BREAD PUDDING, CONCORD GRAPE SAUCE

This is a fantastic fall dish. The great thing about venison is that it has very little fat and is quite good for you. Red cabbage is a classic accompaniment to venison, especially in the Germany-influenced cuisine of France's Alsace region. Baking the cabbage into a savory bread pudding Americanizes the traditional combination. The purple ribbons look beautiful running through the golden currant-studded, clove- and ginger-scented pudding. Baking the cabbage also mellows its somewhat astringent quality, making it accessible to those who may be less fond of its assertive flavor. Concord grapes are in season for a very short period of time, and their delicious, juicy, sweet-tart flavor is a highlight of the season. This sauce calls for Concord grape juice, which is always available, even when the grapes themselves are not.

Serves 8

Bread Pudding

Nonstick cooking spray

½ loaf day-old brioche, cut into 1-inch cubes (about 8 cups)

2 tablespoons extra virgin olive oil

Kosher salt and freshly ground black pepper

3 tablespoons unsalted butter

1 medium red onion, halved and thinly sliced

1 medium head of red cabbage, cored, halved, and finely shredded

2 cups dry red wine, such as Pinot Noir

¼ cup red wine vinegar

¼ cup balsamic vinegar

2 tablespoons sugar

¼ teaspoon plus a pinch of ground cloves

¼ cup dried currants

2 teaspoons honey

3 cups heavy cream

1 teaspoon ground ginger

4 large eggs

Pan-Roasted Venison

3 tablespoons canola oil

8 (8 ounce) venison steaks

Kosher salt and freshly ground black pepper

Concord Grape Sauce (page 158)

Fresh flat-leaf parsley leaves, for garnish

Concord grapes, for garnish

1. To make the bread pudding, preheat the oven to 350°F. Spray the bottom and sides of a 9 x 13-inch baking dish with nonstick cooking spray and set aside.

2. Put the bread cubes on a large baking sheet, toss with the oil, and season with salt and pepper. Bake, turning once, until light golden brown, about 10 minutes. Remove from the oven and let cool.

3. Melt the butter in a large deep sauté pan over high heat. Add the onion and cook until soft, about 4 minutes. Stir in the cabbage and cook for 2 minutes. Add 1 cup water, 1 cup of the wine, both vinegars, the sugar, ¼ teaspoon cloves, and the currants and bring to a boil. Cook until the liquid is reduced by half, about 5 minutes. Reduce the heat to medium, cover the pan, and cook, stirring occasionally, until the cabbage is very tender, about 30 minutes longer. Transfer the cabbage with tongs to a bowl and let cool completely. Reserve the braising liquid.

4. Combine the braising liquid and the remaining 1 cup wine in a small saucepan and bring to a boil over high heat. Cook, stirring occasionally, until it reaches a sauce consistency (see page 250), about 10 minutes. Stir in the honey and season with salt and pepper. Set aside and keep warm.

5. Put the cream, ginger, and pinch of cloves in a small saucepan and bring to a simmer over low heat. Remove from the heat and let cool slightly.

6. Preheat the oven to 350°F.

(recipe continues)

7. Whisk the eggs in a large bowl and slowly whisk in the warm cream. Season with salt and pepper. Add the bread cubes and cabbage to the custard mixture and stir to combine. Press on the bread to submerge it in the custard. Let sit for 15 minutes.

8. Transfer the mixture to the prepared baking dish, cover with foil, and bake for 20 minutes. Remove the foil and bake until the bread pudding is set around the sides but still slightly loose in the center, about 25 minutes longer. Remove from the oven and let sit for 30 minutes before serving.

9. Preheat the oven to 425°F and place a baking sheet on the center rack of the oven.

10. To cook the venison, heat 1½ tablespoons of the oil in a large sauté pan over high heat until it begins to shimmer. Season both sides of 4 of the venison steaks with salt and pepper. Add the steaks to the pan and cook until golden brown and a crust has formed, 3 to 4 minutes. Turn over and cook for 1 minute. Transfer the steaks to a plate and repeat with the remaining 4 steaks and oil.

11. Transfer the steaks to the heated baking sheet and roast in the oven until medium-rare, about 4 minutes. The meat will be red in the center. Remove from the oven and let rest for 5 minutes before slicing.

12. Spoon some of the Concord grape sauce onto large plates and top with the sliced venison. Serve the bread pudding, drizzled with the reserved wine braising liquid, next to the venison. Garnish with parsley leaves and Concord grapes.

CONCORD GRAPE SAUCE
Makes 1½ cups

> 1 quart chicken stock, homemade (page 240) or store-bought
> 2 cups Concord grape juice
> 1 large shallot, chopped
> 2 cloves garlic, coarsely chopped
> 8 black peppercorns
> 8 sprigs fresh thyme

1. Bring the chicken stock to a boil in a medium saucepan over high heat and cook until reduced to 2 cups, about 20 minutes.

2. Meanwhile, combine the grape juice, shallot, garlic, peppercorns, and thyme in a medium saucepan and bring to a boil over high heat. Cook until reduced by half to 1 cup, about 10 minutes.

3. Pour the reduced chicken stock into the reduced grape juice mixture and continue cooking over high heat, stirring occasionally, until reduced to a sauce consistency (see page 250), about 15 minutes. Strain the sauce into a bowl. The sauce can be made 2 days in advance and stored in the refrigerator. Reheat before serving.

GRILLED VENISON CHOPS
BLACKBERRY-SAGE BROWN BUTTER

Both venison and blackberries are farmed these days, but they were once procured in the wild, by early American hunters and foragers. I like to think that this dish is one that would have been at home—in essence if not preparation—on the table of pioneers first settling the woods of northern Wisconsin and Michigan. Blackberries have a tart edge to their fruity flavor, which enlivens the richness of nutty brown butter. The sauce is hit with just a hint of sage, and its slightly woodsy flavor brings out the still-wild-at-heart nature of the berries. Sage is a potent herb, and you need to employ it in small doses. If you can't find or aren't a fan of venison, lamb or even pork chops would work in its place.

Serves 4

4 (8-ounce, 1½-inch-thick) venison chops
2 tablespoons canola oil
Kosher salt and freshly ground black pepper
12 tablespoons (1½ sticks) unsalted butter, cut into pieces
4 fresh sage leaves, cut into thin strips, plus whole leaves for garnish
12 fresh blackberries, sliced in half

1. Preheat the grill to high or heat a grill pan over high heat.

2. Brush both sides of the chops with the oil and season with salt and pepper. Put on the grill and grill until golden brown and slightly charred, about 4 minutes. Reduce the heat to medium, flip the chops, and continue cooking until cooked to medium-rare, about 8 minutes longer. Transfer to a platter, tent loosely with foil, and let rest for 5 minutes before serving.

3. While the venison is resting, melt the butter in a medium sauté pan over medium-low heat. Add the sliced sage leaves and cook, occasionally stirring and turning the leaves, until the edges curl and the butter is dark amber but not black or burned, about 5 minutes. Add the blackberries to the butter and cook for 20 seconds. Season with salt and pepper.

4. Spoon some of the butter onto 4 large plates, top with the veal chops, and spoon some of the blackberries and butter over each chop. Garnish with fresh sage leaves.

SIDES

BROOKLYN HASH BROWNS

You could certainly serve these hash browns with eggs, but I didn't find the inspiration for this dish at my local diner. These belong right next to a juicy steak. I mix sweet caramelized onions with cooked potatoes seasoned with smoky paprika. Cooked in butter and oil, the bottom layer of potatoes becomes amazingly crisp and is browned to perfection. Serve this bottom side up so that everyone can see what crispy potato goodness awaits.

Serves 4

4 tablespoons (½ stick) unsalted butter

2 tablespoons canola oil

2 large Spanish onions, halved and thinly sliced

Kosher salt and freshly ground black pepper

2 pounds Idaho potatoes, peeled and cut
    into 1-inch dice

2 teaspoons smoked sweet Spanish paprika

2 tablespoons finely chopped fresh chives

1. Heat 1 tablespoon of the butter and 1 tablespoon of the oil in a medium sauté pan over medium heat. Add the onions and cook, stirring occasionally, until golden brown and caramelized, about 40 minutes. Season with salt and pepper.

2. Meanwhile, put the potatoes in a medium pot of salted cold water. Bring to a boil and cook until the potatoes are nearly tender and a knife inserted into the centers still meets a little resistance, 10 to 12 minutes. Drain well.

3. Combine the onions and potatoes in a bowl, add the paprika, and season with salt and pepper. Divide the mixture into 8 portions, forming each into a ½-inch-thick rectangle.

4. Heat the remaining 3 tablespoons butter and 1 tablespoon oil on a cast-iron griddle or in a large nonstick sauté pan over medium heat. Add the potato rectangles and cook until the undersides are golden brown, about 10 minutes. Flip them over with a spatula and cook until the bottoms are pale golden brown and just set, about 2 minutes.

5. Serve 2 hash browns per person, garnished with the chives.

BARBECUED POTATO CHIPS

We serve these chips, an all-American classic, with our Lobster Club (page 50) for lunch at Bar Americain, but you could serve them with any sandwich—or just sit in front of the TV and eat a big bowl of them on their own. Making your own potato chips and seasoning does require a little work, but the end result is definitely worth it. That said, if you don't want to make homemade potato chips, you can substitute your favorite brand of plain potato chips, spread them in an even layer on a baking sheet, and heat in a 325°F oven for 5 minutes before tossing them in the barbecue seasoning.

Serves 4 to 6

1 tablespoon smoked sweet Spanish paprika

2 teaspoons ground ancho chile

2 teaspoons ground cumin

2 teaspoons kosher salt

1 teaspoon onion powder

1 teaspoon garlic powder

1 teaspoon light brown sugar

1 teaspoon freshly ground black pepper

3 large Idaho potatoes, peeled and sliced
    lengthwise ⅛ inch thick on a mandoline

2 quarts peanut or canola oil

1. Mix together the paprika, ground ancho, cumin, salt, onion and garlic powders, brown sugar, and pepper in a small bowl.

2. Place the potato slices on a baking sheet between layers of paper towels to make sure they are very dry before frying.

3. Heat the oil in a large saucepan until it reaches 375°F on a deep-fat thermometer. Fry the potatoes in small batches until golden brown on both sides, turning once, 1½ minutes total. Remove with a slotted spoon and place on a brown paper bag or another baking sheet lined with paper towels to drain. Season immediately with the barbecue seasoning.

FRIES AMERICAIN
SMOKED RED PEPPER MAYONNAISE

Dipping French fries in mayonnaise is a European conceit. The French and Belgians wouldn't serve their *pommes frites* with anything else! If you haven't given it a try, you should—the combination of hot, crisp, salty fries and smooth, rich mayonnaise is dangerously addictive. I dust these fries with a healthy dose of spicy black pepper before sending them out of Bar Americain's kitchen. The familiar spice has quite a kick, the level of which you can adjust to suit your taste. The smoked red pepper mayonnaise is richly flavored with smoky chipotle in adobo and sweet roasted red pepper. The mayonnaise comes together in an instant in the food processor. Try it on your favorite sandwich, as a dip for veggies, with fish . . . all it takes is one dip and you'll find yourself whipping it up time and time again.

Serves 4

1 cup mayonnaise
1 red bell pepper, roasted, peeled, seeded, and chopped (see page 250)
1 or 2 canned chipotles in adobo, depending on how spicy you like it
Kosher salt and freshly ground black pepper
5 large Idaho potatoes, peeled
1 quart canola or peanut oil

1. Combine the mayonnaise, red pepper, chipotle, 1 teaspoon salt, and ¼ teaspoon pepper in a food processor and process until smooth.

2. Cut the potatoes into ¼-inch-thick slices, then cut each slice into ¼-inch-thick fries. Submerge the fries in a large bowl of cold water.

3. Heat the oil in a large, deep, straight-sided skillet until it reaches 325°F on a deep-fat thermometer. Drain the fries in batches on paper towels. Fry each batch until a pale blonde color, 3 to 4 minutes. Transfer to a baking sheet lined with paper towels.

4. Raise the heat of the oil to 375°F and fry the potatoes again, in batches, until golden brown, 3 to 4 minutes. Transfer to a baking sheet lined with paper towels and season with salt and a generous grinding of pepper.

5. Serve the hot fries with the smoked red pepper mayonnaise on the side for dipping.

LOBSTER POTATO SALAD

I don't know why people seem surprised by this one; it makes perfect sense to me! Lobster and potatoes have each been the starring ingredient in their own salads for ages—in this recipe, they share double billing, resulting in a dish that is infinitely better than either of the individual salads that inspired it. Besides the lobster, thin-skinned and buttery fingerling potatoes give the potato salad a major upgrade. The mayonnaise-based dressing features a blend of pungent horseradish, Dijon mustard, and bright lemon juice. I love anise-flavored tarragon with lobster; its delicate leaves are folded in along with lemony parsley right before serving.

Serves 4 to 6

1½ pounds medium fingerling potatoes, scrubbed

Kosher salt

¾ cup mayonnaise

2 tablespoons red wine vinegar

2 tablespoons fresh lemon juice

2 tablespoons prepared horseradish, drained

2 tablespoons whole grain mustard

1 tablespoon Dijon mustard

1 tablespoon honey

Freshly ground black pepper

1 pound cooked fresh lobster meat, coarsely chopped

2 tablespoons finely chopped fresh tarragon

¼ cup chopped fresh flat-leaf parsley

1. Put the potatoes in a large pot and add enough cold water to cover. Add 1 tablespoon salt and bring to a boil over high heat. Cook until the potatoes are tender when pierced with a knife, 12 to 15 minutes. Drain well, let cool slightly, and then cut crosswise into ¼-inch-thick slices. Put the potatoes in a large bowl and cover with aluminum foil to keep them warm while you prepare the dressing.

2. Whisk together the mayonnaise, vinegar, lemon juice, horseradish, mustards, and honey in a small bowl and season with salt and pepper. Pour over the potatoes, add the lobster, tarragon, and parsley, and fold gently to combine. Season with salt and pepper. The salad can be refrigerated for up to 8 hours. It is best served at room temperature.

SWEET POTATO GRATIN

Definitely decadent, this sweet potato gratin is destined to become a standard part of your family's holiday spread. Cinnamon, clove, and nutmeg perfume the cream with their warm flavors and seep their rich taste of fall into each layer. A mandoline makes quick work of slicing the potatoes and is worth the investment for the time it will save you in prep work. Don't forget to remove the cover for the last portion of baking time—the browned and bubbling crust is not to be missed!

Serves 8

2 cups heavy cream
1¼ teaspoons ground cinnamon
¼ teaspoon ground cloves
¼ teaspoon freshly grated nutmeg
4 medium sweet potatoes, peeled and sliced
⅛ inch thick on a mandoline
Kosher salt and freshly ground black pepper

1. Preheat the oven to 375°F.

2. Whisk together the cream, cinnamon, cloves, and nutmeg until smooth.

3. In a 10-inch square baking dish, arrange an even layer of sweet potatoes. Drizzle with a few table-spoons of the cream mixture and season with salt and pepper. Repeat with the remaining potatoes and cream, seasoning with salt and pepper, to form 8 to 10 layers. Press down on the layers to totally submerge the sweet potatoes in the cream mixture.

4. Cover and bake for 30 minutes. Remove the cover and continue baking until the cream has been absorbed, the potatoes are cooked through, and the top is browned, 30 to 45 minutes. Remove from the oven and let rest for 15 minutes before serving.

GREEN PEA COUSCOUS

Light and fresh, this couscous can be served hot as a side dish for any number of entrees, or at room temperature as you would any other pasta- or grain-based salad. Israeli couscous is a small, round semolina pasta resembling barley or large tapioca pearls. Traditional couscous is much smaller and is soaked rather than boiled; I prefer Israeli couscous for its uniform shape and its firm yet tender texture. Diced roasted red pepper and sweet green peas deliver a pop of color to the pearly couscous. Mildly assertive green onions balance the peas' and pepper's sweetness, as do tart lemon juice and its bright zest. Pine nuts, toasted to deepen their flavor, add their crunchy yet creamy texture to the mix.

Serves 4 to 6

½ pound (1½ cups) Israeli couscous
3 tablespoons unsalted butter
1 teaspoon finely grated lemon zest
Juice of 1 lemon
1 teaspoon honey
2 cups frozen peas, thawed
1 red bell pepper, roasted, peeled, seeded,
and finely diced (see page 250)
3 green onions, green and pale green parts,
thinly sliced
3 tablespoons pine nuts, toasted (see page 250)
¼ cup finely chopped fresh flat-leaf parsley
Kosher salt and freshly ground black pepper

1. Bring 2 quarts of salted water to a boil in a large saucepan. Add the couscous and cook until al dente, about 8 minutes. Drain well in a colander.

2. Melt the butter in a large sauté pan over medium heat. Stir in the zest, lemon juice, and honey and cook for 30 seconds. Add the couscous, peas, and red pepper and cook until heated through, about 2 minutes. Stir in the green onions, pine nuts, and parsley and season with salt and pepper. Serve hot or at room temperature.

CREAMED KALE
CRISPY SHALLOTS

Let this be the dish to make a kale lover out of you. If you are a fan of creamed spinach, there is no way you won't fall head over heels for this dish. The same luscious flavors are all in play; the creamy sauce is spiked with onion, garlic, and a touch of nutmeg. Changing the leafy green from spinach to kale is a seemingly small substitute with a big impact. Like spinach, kale is packed with nutrients, but unlike spinach, it doesn't melt into the sauce; its texture is sturdier and retains its body when cooked. Crispy shallots bring another layer of texture along with their mild onion flavor.

Serves 6 to 8

3 pounds kale, stems and ribs removed, coarsely chopped
3½ cups whole milk, or more if needed
3 tablespoons unsalted butter, plus more for the baking dish
1 medium Spanish onion, finely diced
3 cloves garlic, finely chopped
3 tablespoons all-purpose flour
⅛ teaspoon freshly grated nutmeg
Kosher salt and freshly ground black pepper
Crispy Shallots (recipe follows)

1. Preheat the oven to 350°F. Butter a 10-inch square baking dish.

2. Bring a large pot of salted water to a boil. Add the kale and cook until tender, about 5 minutes. Drain in a colander, rinse with cold water, and drain well again. Place the kale in clean kitchen towels or paper towels and squeeze out the excess liquid. Put the kale in a large bowl.

3. Pour the milk into a medium saucepan and bring to a simmer over low heat.

4. Melt the butter in a medium saucepan over medium-high heat. Add the onion and cook until soft, about 4 minutes. Add the garlic and cook for 30 seconds. Whisk in the flour and cook until smooth and light blonde in color, about 1 minute. Slowly whisk in the warm milk, raise the heat to high, and cook, whisking constantly, until thickened and the flour taste has cooked out, about 5 minutes. If the mixture becomes too thick, add a little more milk.

5. Strain the sauce over the kale. Add the nutmeg, season with salt and pepper, and mix gently to combine. Scrape the mixture into the baking dish and bake in the oven until light golden brown on top and just warmed through, about 15 minutes.

6. Remove from the oven and top with the crispy shallots. Let rest for 10 minutes before serving.

CRISPY SHALLOTS
Serves 6 to 8 as a garnish

2 cups canola oil
1 cup all-purpose flour
Kosher salt and freshly ground black pepper
6 large shallots, sliced into thin rings

1. Heat the oil in a medium saucepan until it reaches 360°F on a deep-fat thermometer.

2. Put the flour on a large plate and season with salt and pepper. Working in batches, dredge the shallots in the flour. Transfer them to a large slotted spoon or spider and tap off the excess flour. Fry the shallots in batches, stirring a few times, until light golden brown and crisp, 30 to 45 seconds. Transfer with a slotted spoon to a plate lined with paper towels and season with salt and pepper.

CREAMED CORN

One of the first images that comes to mind when I think of the Midwest is that of endless green corn fields, this comforting side dish was born in the home kitchens of that region. If your memory of creamed corn has been tainted by a run-in with a bland, mushy, straight-from-the can version, you owe it to yourself take a fresh look at the real deal. Sweet corn kernels are mixed into a creamy béchamel sauce flavored with onions and garlic and cooked until just tender. The sauce is absorbed by the corn and plumps the kernels (even frozen ones) so that they practically pop in every mouthful. Roasted red peppers and green poblanos add both color and a savory counterpoint to the naturally sweet corn.

Serves 4 to 6

2 cups whole milk, or more if needed

2 tablespoons unsalted butter

1 small Spanish onion, finely diced

2 cloves garlic, finely chopped

2 tablespoons all-purpose flour

1 red bell pepper, roasted, peeled, seeded, and finely diced (see page 250)

1 small poblano chile, roasted, peeled, seeded, and finely diced (see page 250)

4 cups fresh or thawed frozen corn kernels

Kosher salt and freshly ground black pepper

1. Pour the milk into a small saucepan and bring to a simmer over low heat.

2. Melt the butter in a medium saucepan over medium-high heat. Add the onion and cook until soft, about 4 minutes. Add the garlic and cook for 30 seconds. Stir in the flour and cook until pale blonde in color, about 1 minute.

3. Whisk in the hot milk, raise the heat to high, and cook, whisking constantly, until the mixture is thickened and coats the back of a spoon, 3 to 4 minutes. If the mixture is too thick, whisk in a little more milk, a few tablespoons at a time.

4. Reduce the heat to low, add the red pepper, poblano, and corn, and cook until the corn is tender, about 10 minutes for fresh corn and 4 minutes for frozen. Season with salt and pepper.

ROASTED ASPARAGUS
GREEN PEPPERCORN VINAIGRETTE

Brine-packed green peppercorns have a sharp, fresh, and somewhat fruity flavor that is less pungent than you might imagine coming from a peppercorn. Roasting asparagus to crisp-tender deepens its "green" flavor, and the dark blisters it acquires in the oven are especially tasty. Asparagus has a distinctive flavor, and this vinaigrette walks a delicate line, standing up to that flavor without overwhelming it. This simple side is a favorite of diners at Bar Americain.

Serves 4

3 tablespoons white wine vinegar

1 tablespoon Dijon mustard

2 teaspoons honey

Kosher salt and freshly ground black pepper

¼ cup plus 2 tablespoons extra virgin olive oil

2 tablespoons green peppercorns in brine,
   drained

1 pound fresh asparagus, trimmed

Chopped fresh flat-leaf parsley leaves,
   for garnish

1. Whisk together the vinegar, mustard, and honey in a small bowl until combined. Season with salt and pepper. Slowly whisk in ¼ cup of the olive oil until emulsified and stir in the peppercorns. Let the vinaigrette sit at room temperature for 15 minutes or refrigerate for up to 8 hours. Bring to room temperature before serving.

2. Preheat the oven to 375°F.

3. Scatter the asparagus on a rimmed baking sheet, toss with the remaining 2 tablespoons oil, and season with salt and pepper. Roast in the oven until just cooked through, about 8 minutes.

4. Transfer the asparagus to a platter, drizzle the vinaigrette over the top, and garnish with parsley.

SMOKED CHILE COLLARD GREENS

Collard greens are a point of southern pride. Any barbecue or soul food restaurant worth its salt has a place for these mustardy-flavored greens. In the South, collard greens are typically cooked with a ham hock or smoked turkey wings to give a great smoky flavor to the greens and the broth—or pot liquor as it is referred to in local parlance. You can definitely add either to this recipe, but I like to use chipotle chiles to give not only smokiness but also a little heat to this dish. I prefer my collard greens to retain some bite and cook them until tender, not to melting. The greens have a natural sweetness that is both accentuated and balanced by the finishing splash of apple cider vinegar. Sweet, smoky, and slightly vinegary, these collard greens definitely deliver a touch of soul to the table.

Serves 4

2 tablespoons canola oil

1 medium Spanish onion, finely diced

4 cloves garlic, finely chopped

2 to 3 teaspoons pureed canned chipotle chiles in adobo, to taste

2½ pounds collard greens, stems and ribs removed, coarsely chopped

Kosher salt and freshly ground black pepper

3 tablespoons apple cider vinegar

1. Heat the oil in a large deep sauté pan over high heat until the oil begins to shimmer. Add the onion and cook until soft, about 4 minutes. Add the garlic and cook for 1 minute.

2. Add 1½ cups water and the chipotle puree and bring to a boil. Add the collards, season with salt and pepper, and turn to coat in the mixture. Reduce the heat to low, cover the pot, and cook, stirring occasionally, until the greens are crisp-tender, 15 to 20 minutes. Transfer to a platter and drizzle with the vinegar.

ROASTED BRUSSELS SPROUTS
POMEGRANATE, HAZELNUTS

Brussels sprouts used to be up there with lima beans on the list of vegetables people claimed to hate, but I think they're having an overdue resurgence in popularity. These roasted Brussels sprouts are tender yet firm and have a wonderful nutty, earthy flavor. Rich hazelnuts add texture, as does the tart pop of garnet-colored pomegranate seeds. This is a beautiful fall side dish.

Serves 4 to 6

1¼ pounds Brussels sprouts, trimmed and halved
2 tablespoons canola oil
Kosher salt and freshly ground black pepper
3 tablespoons pomegranate molasses
Seeds from 1 pomegranate
½ cup coarsely chopped toasted (see page 250) hazelnuts
Finely grated zest of 1 lime
1 tablespoon finely grated orange zest

1. Preheat the oven to 375°F.

2. Put the Brussels sprouts in a medium roasting pan, toss with the oil, and season with salt and pepper. Roast in the oven until light golden brown and a knife inserted into the centers goes in without any resistance, about 45 minutes.

3. Transfer the sprouts to a large bowl and add the pomegranate molasses, pomegranate seeds, hazelnuts, and lime and orange zests. Season with salt as needed.

VARIATION
ROASTED BRUSSELS SPROUTS
VANILLA PECAN BUTTER

Split a vanilla bean lengthwise and scrape out the seeds. Combine 6 tablespoons (¾ stick) unsalted butter, softened, with the vanilla bean seeds in a small bowl. Fold in ¼ cup finely chopped toasted pecans and season with salt and pepper to taste. Cover and refrigerate for at least 30 minutes or up to 2 days before serving. Remove from the refrigerator to soften slightly for 20 minutes before using.

Roast the Brussels sprouts as directed, omitting the pomegranate molasses, pomegranate seeds, hazelnuts, and lime and orange zests. Remove the Brussels sprouts from the oven and immediately toss with the vanilla pecan butter.

CAULIFLOWER AND GOAT CHEESE GRATIN

Warm and bubbly with a golden brown crust, this easy-to-prepare side dish is one of my favorite cold-weather indulgences. I am a big fan of cauliflower's soft, slightly nutty flavor and don't think it gets the attention it deserves. It has a remarkable ability to absorb the flavors of whatever it is being cooked with, such as the rich creamy sauce of smooth Monterey Jack, salty Parmesan, and tangy goat cheeses in this gratin.

Serves 4 to 6

2 tablespoons unsalted butter, plus more for the baking dish

3 cups whole milk, or more if needed

2 tablespoons all-purpose flour

6 ounces Monterey Jack cheese, grated (1½ cups)

6 ounces fresh goat cheese, cut into small pieces

½ cup freshly grated Parmesan cheese

Kosher salt and freshly ground black pepper

1 medium head of cauliflower, cut into florets, each floret cut into 2 or 3 pieces

Chopped fresh flat-leaf parsley, for garnish

1. Preheat the oven to 350°F and butter a 10-inch baking dish.

2. Pour the milk into a small saucepan and bring to a simmer over medium-low heat.

3. Melt the butter over medium heat in a medium heavy saucepan. Whisk in the flour and cook for 1 minute; do not let the mixture brown. Slowly whisk in the milk, raise the heat to high, and cook, whisking constantly, until the mixture thickens, 3 to 4 minutes. Remove from the heat and whisk in the Monterey Jack, half of the goat cheese, and half of the Parmesan cheese. Season with salt and pepper. If the mixture seems too thick, thin with a little extra milk.

4. Transfer the sauce to a large bowl, add the cauliflower, and stir well to combine. Scrape the mixture into the prepared baking dish and top with the remaining goat cheese and Parmesan. Slip a rimmed baking sheet underneath and bake until the cauliflower is tender and the top is bubbly and golden brown, 50 to 60 minutes. Remove from the oven and let rest for 10 minutes before serving. Garnish with chopped parsley.

CRANBERRY, FIG, AND PINOT NOIR CHUTNEY

Cranberries are transformed with sweet, subtly earthy dried figs and velvety, slightly spicy Pinot Noir into a chunky, jamlike chutney. Orange zest infuses the mix with its bright citrus flavor and essential oils. Ginger works well in both savory and sweet preparations, and its touch of heat bridges the wine and fruit here. You can serve this chutney instead of the standard cranberry sauce at Thanksgiving, but it is also wonderful with pork and venison dishes, spread on a sandwich, or as an accompaniment to a cheese plate.

Makes about 4 cups

1½ cups Pinot Noir

12 dried figs, diced

¾ cup sugar

3 strips orange zest

1 (2-inch) piece fresh ginger, peeled
   and finely grated

4 cups fresh or frozen cranberries

Kosher salt and freshly ground black pepper

1. Bring the wine to a simmer in a small saucepan. Remove from the heat, add the figs, and let soak until soft, about 30 minutes. Drain, reserving the wine and figs separately.

2. Combine the sugar, 1½ cups water, the reserved wine, orange zest, and ginger in a large saucepan and bring to a boil over high heat. Cook until the sugar has completely melted, a minute or two. Add half of the cranberries and cook, stirring occasionally, until the berries have popped and are very soft, about 10 minutes. Stir in the remaining cranberries and the soaked figs and cook for 5 minutes longer. Season lightly with salt and pepper.

3. Discard the orange zest and scrape the chutney into a serving bowl. Serve at room temperature or chilled. The chutney can be prepared 24 hours in advance and stored covered in the refrigerator.

BARBECUED BAKED BEANS
HONEY, DOUBLE-SMOKED BACON

What could be more American than a pot of baked beans? From "Beantown's" own Boston baked beans to one of the South's favorite sides for a plate of barbecue, baked beans are an integral part of our culinary heritage. Molasses is a traditional ingredient here; its dark, rich flavor and thick texture give the dish its characteristic sweetness and consistency. I use a little less than most folks and supplement it with a generous dose of honey to mellow it out and allow the rest of the flavorings—dark rum and barbecue sauce among them—to shine. My southwestern culinary leanings are what prompt me to use black beans. I like their somewhat firm texture, but you could certainly use traditional navy beans if you'd prefer. The fat and smoky flavor of bacon is essential. Double-smoked bacon gives you even more of that amazing taste.

Serves 8

1 pound dried black beans, picked over
1 tablespoon canola oil
½ pound thick double-smoked bacon, cut into small dice
1 medium Spanish onion, cut into small dice
1 medium carrot, cut into small dice
4 cloves garlic, finely chopped
1 cup dark rum
¼ cup honey
2 tablespoons molasses
1½ cups chicken stock, homemade (page 240) or store-bought, plus more if needed
1½ cups Mesa Grill Barbecue Sauce (see Sources) or store-bought barbecue sauce
½ cup coarsely chopped fresh cilantro
Kosher salt and freshly ground black pepper

1. Cover the beans by at least 2 inches with cold water and let soak for at least 8 hours or overnight.

2. Drain the beans, place in a large saucepan, and cover by 2 inches with cold water. Bring to a boil over high heat, reduce the heat to medium, cover the pot slightly, and cook until very tender, 1 to 1½ hours. Drain the beans and place in a large bowl.

3. Preheat the oven to 325°F.

4. Heat the oil in a large sauté pan over high heat. Add the bacon and cook until golden brown and crisp, about 8 minutes. Transfer with a slotted spoon to a plate lined with paper towels. Add the onion and carrot to the pan and cook until soft, about 5 minutes. Add the garlic and cook for 1 minute. Add the rum, bring to a boil, and cook until almost completely evaporated, 5 minutes. Add the mixture to the beans along with the honey, molasses, stock, barbecue sauce, bacon, and half of the cilantro. Season with salt and pepper and mix gently to combine.

5. Transfer the mixture to a 10-inch round baking dish, cover, and bake for 20 minutes. Check to see if the mixture is dry; if it is, add a little more stock. Continue baking for another 20 minutes. Remove the lid and bake until golden brown on top, another 15 minutes.

6. Remove from the oven and let sit for 10 minutes. Garnish with the remaining cilantro before serving.

GREEN CHILE SPOONBREAD

For those of you who are not from the South, spoonbread is best described as a cross between a soufflé and corn bread. Light and creamy like a soufflé, this elegant side dish delivers the essence of corn bread without any of its density. Parmesan cheese gives the spoonbread a rich, savory note, while sweet roasted garlic and roasted green chiles provide the force of its flavor profile. Chopped chives and oregano fleck each bite with fresh color and flavor. At Bar Americain we serve Green Chile Spoonbread alongside the Smoked Chicken with Black Pepper Vinegar Sauce (page 126), but I would be hard-pressed to think of a meal that wouldn't be complemented by this dish.

Serves 8 to 10

2 tablespoons unsalted butter, softened

¾ cup freshly grated Parmesan cheese

3 cups whole milk

1½ cups fine yellow cornmeal

6 large eggs, separated

1½ cups buttermilk

6 cloves roasted garlic (see page 250), finely chopped

2 teaspoons baking powder

¾ teaspoon baking soda

1½ tablespoons kosher salt

1 teaspoon cayenne

3 Hatch or 2 medium poblano or Anaheim chiles, roasted, peeled, seeded, and finely diced (see page 250)

2 tablespoons finely chopped fresh oregano

½ cup finely chopped fresh chives

1 tablespoon sugar

1. Preheat the oven to 350°F. Grease the bottom and sides of a 12-inch square baking dish with the butter and sprinkle with ¼ cup of the Parmesan cheese.

2. Bring the milk to a boil in a small saucepan. Put the cornmeal in a large bowl and whisk in the hot milk. Let cool for a few minutes before whisking in the egg yolks. Add the buttermilk, garlic, baking powder, baking soda, salt, cayenne, roasted chiles, oregano, and chives and mix until combined.

3. Whip the egg whites in an electric mixer fitted with the whisk attachment until frothy. Slowly add the sugar and continue whipping until soft peaks form. Fold the egg whites into the cornmeal mixture and spread evenly in the prepared baking dish.

4. Sprinkle the remaining ½ cup Parmesan evenly over the top of the batter and bake until the top is golden brown and the inside is soft and fluffy, about 40 minutes. Cut into squares and serve hot.

SOURDOUGH, WILD MUSHROOM, AND BACON DRESSING

I grew up calling any side dish of seasoned, moistened, and baked bread cubes "stuffing," but I've been corrected enough times to have changed my ways: If it goes inside the turkey or chicken, it's stuffing. If it's cooked in a dish of its very own, it's officially dressing. As it so happens, I like to serve this side with more than just poultry, and I especially love the browned crust, so dressing it is! Two other key factors in delivering dynamic texture are to toast the cubes of tangy sourdough bread first and to use a combination of thinly sliced and coarsely chopped mushrooms. Roasting the mushrooms before mixing with the other ingredients heightens their deep earthy flavor while cooking off any excess liquid. Studded with salty bits of bacon and fresh herbs, this side dish is destined to become a favorite of your Thanksgiving—or any dinner—table.

Serves 8

Unsalted butter, for the baking dish
1¼ pounds sourdough bread, crusts trimmed, cut into ½-inch cubes (about 12 cups)
½ pound shiitake mushrooms, stemmed and coarsely chopped
½ pound oyster mushrooms, coarsely chopped
1 pound cremini mushrooms, thinly sliced
4 tablespoons canola oil
Kosher salt and freshly ground black pepper
¾ pound slab bacon, cut into ½-inch dice
1 large Spanish onion, finely diced
5 cloves garlic, finely chopped
4 to 6 cups chicken stock, homemade (page 240) or store-bought, as needed
2 tablespoons finely chopped fresh sage
2 tablespoons finely chopped fresh thyme
½ cup chopped fresh flat-leaf parsley
2 large eggs

1. Preheat the oven to 350°F. Butter a 13 x 9 x 2-inch glass baking dish.

2. Spread the bread on a large baking sheet (or 2 smaller baking sheets) in an even layer and bake, stirring a few times, until light golden brown, about 12 minutes. Remove from the oven and let cool. Put the cubes into a very large bowl.

3. Raise the oven temperature to 375°F.

4. Combine the mushrooms in a large baking dish or rimmed baking sheet, toss with 3 tablespoons of the oil, and season with salt and pepper. Roast in the oven, stirring several times, until soft and golden brown, about 30 minutes.

5. While the mushrooms are roasting, heat the remaining 1 tablespoon oil in a large deep sauté pan over medium heat. Add the bacon and cook, stirring occasionally, until golden brown and the fat has rendered, about 10 minutes. Transfer the bacon with a slotted spoon to a plate lined with paper towels.

6. Pour off all but 2 tablespoons of the rendered fat in the sauté pan and return to the stove over high heat. Add the onion and cook until soft, about 4 minutes. Add the garlic and cook for 1 minute. Add 3 cups of the chicken stock, the sage, thyme, and parsley and season with salt and pepper. Bring to a simmer.

7. Add the mushrooms to the bread. Whisk the eggs in a small bowl and then whisk in a few tablespoons of the warm stock mixture. Add the eggs and the rest of the stock mixture to the bread, season with salt and pepper, and stir to combine. The dressing should be very wet; add more stock as needed. Scrape the mixture into the prepared baking dish. Cover with foil and bake for 25 minutes. Remove the foil and continue baking until the top is golden brown, 25 to 30 minutes longer. Remove from the oven and let cool for 10 minutes before serving.

BREADS AND DESSERTS

BLACK PEPPER BUTTERMILK BISCUITS

These are everything a good buttermilk biscuit should be: light, flaky, and exceedingly tender. They make appearances all over the menu at Bar Americain; they're a fought-over item in our bread basket, the basis of Miss Stephanie's Biscuits and Cream Gravy (page 223), and when I'm not feeling the waffles, the perfect accompaniment for fried chicken (page 131). A liberal dusting of black pepper gives the biscuits a subtle flush of heat that distinguishes them from the rest. The purists among you can leave out this last step if you prefer your biscuits free of adornment—they're still melt-in-your-mouth good.

Makes 10 to 12

4 cups all-purpose flour, plus more for shaping
1 tablespoon plus 1 teaspoon baking powder
1 teaspoon baking soda
1 teaspoon fine salt
12 tablespoons (1½ sticks) unsalted butter, cut into small pieces, chilled, plus 4 tablespoons (½ stick), melted
1½ cups buttermilk, chilled
½ cup heavy cream
2 teaspoons freshly ground black pepper

1. Preheat the oven to 450°F. Line a large baking sheet with parchment paper.

2. Combine the flour, baking powder, baking soda, and salt in a large bowl. Cut in the cold butter using your fingers or a pastry cutter until the mixture resembles coarse meal. Add the buttermilk and mix gently until the mixture just begins to come together.

3. Scrape the dough onto a lightly floured counter. Pat the dough into a 10 x 12-inch rectangle about ¾ inch thick. Use a 2-inch round cutter to cut out biscuits. Press together the scraps of dough and repeat to cut 10 to 12 biscuits total.

4. Place the biscuits 2 inches apart on the baking sheet, brush the tops with the cream, and sprinkle with the black pepper. Bake the biscuits until light golden brown, 12 to 15 minutes. Brush the biscuits with the melted butter and transfer them to a wire rack to cool at least slightly.

TOMATO CORN BREAD

This corn bread has an unusual twist. In many ways, it is a very traditional recipe made with stone-ground yellow cornmeal, tangy buttermilk for moisture, and just a touch of sugar so that it is savory rather than sweet. Cooked in a cast-iron skillet, the inner crumb is tender and crumbly while the bottom crust is beautifully crisp. What elevates this corn bread beyond the norm is that mystery ingredient—tomato powder. I can't imagine how many tomatoes it takes to make even a couple tablespoons of the powder, but the flavor and scent are unadulterated, concentrated tomato essence. The powder mixes evenly into the batter, and each bite is laced with its pure taste.

Makes 1 (9-inch) round corn bread

1½ cups stone-ground yellow cornmeal
½ cup all-purpose flour
2 tablespoons sugar
½ teaspoon baking powder
½ teaspoon baking soda
1¼ teaspoons fine salt
¼ teaspoon freshly ground black pepper
2 large eggs
3 tablespoons tomato powder (see Sources)
1½ cups buttermilk
8 tablespoons (1 stick) unsalted butter, melted
Nonstick cooking spray

1. Heat a dry cast-iron skillet in the lower third of the oven while preheating the oven to 425°F.

2. Whisk together the cornmeal, flour, sugar, baking powder, baking soda, salt, and pepper in a bowl.

3. Whisk together the eggs, tomato powder, and buttermilk in a bowl. Add to the flour mixture with the melted butter and whisk until just combined.

4. Carefully remove the hot pan from the oven and spray the bottom and sides with nonstick cooking spray. Scrape the batter into the pan and bake until light golden brown and a tester inserted into the center comes out with a few moist crumbs, about 18 minutes. Unmold and let cool slightly on a wire rack before cutting into pieces and serving.

CORN BREAD STICKS

Served as part of the bread basket at Bar Amercain, these hot-from-the-oven corn sticks are one of the recipes requested most by diners.

Makes 14

3 tablespoons canola oil
1 tablespoon unsalted butter, plus 4 tablespoons (½ stick), melted and cooled
2 large shallots, finely diced
1 cup coarse yellow cornmeal
1 cup all-purpose flour
2 tablespoons sugar
2½ teaspoons baking powder
½ teaspoon baking soda
1 teaspoon fine salt
¼ teaspoon freshly ground black pepper
1¼ cups buttermilk, at room temperature, plus more if needed
2 large eggs

1. Preheat the oven to 425°F. Brush cast-iron corn stick molds with 2 tablespoons of the canola oil and place in the oven on baking sheets.

2. Melt the 1 tablespoon butter with the remaining 1 tablespoon canola oil in a small sauté pan over medium heat. Add the shallots and cook, stirring occasionally, until golden brown and caramelized, about 10 minutes. Remove from the heat and let cool slightly.

3. Stir together the cornmeal, flour, sugar, baking powder, baking soda, salt, and pepper in a large bowl.

4. Whisk together the buttermilk, melted butter, and eggs in a small bowl. Add to the flour mixture along with the shallots and mix until just combined. Add more buttermilk if necessary to thin to just pourable consistency.

5. Carefully remove the hot molds from the oven and fill each mold to the top with some of the batter. Bake the corn sticks until light golden brown and a toothpick inserted into the centers comes out with a few moist crumbs, about 20 minutes. Remove from the oven and let cool in the pans for 10 minutes before unmolding. Using the tip of small sharp knife, gently lift the corn sticks from the molds. Serve warm.

CHIPOTLE BRIOCHE

This rich, buttery bread, spiked with a bit of smoky heat, is the perfect complement to the sweet lobster salad in the Lobster Club (page 50) and the sharp cheeses and green tomatoes in the Grilled Cheese (page 49). It's also great just sliced and served as part of your dinner bread basket.

Makes 1 (13-inch) loaf

1 envelope active dry yeast

2 tablespoons sugar

1¼ cups whole milk, warmed

8 cups all-purpose flour, plus more for shaping

2 tablespoons kosher salt

2 large eggs

7 large egg yolks

¼ cup pureed canned chipotle chiles in adobo

¾ pound (3 sticks) unsalted butter, cut into pieces, slightly softened, plus more for the bowl, pan, and loaf

1. Combine the yeast, sugar, and warm milk in a small bowl and let sit until foamy, about 5 minutes.

2. In the bowl of a stand mixer fitted with the dough hook, combine the flour and salt. Mixing on low speed, add the yeast mixture and mix until combined. In a separate bowl, whisk together the eggs, egg yolks, and chipotle puree and then slowly add the mixture to the flour while continuing to mix on low speed. Mix in the butter, piece by piece, until combined. Continue mixing until the dough is silky and springy, about 10 minutes.

3. Transfer the dough to a lightly floured surface and knead lightly for 30 seconds. Place in a lightly greased bowl, cover with a clean kitchen towel or plastic wrap, and let rise in a warm place until doubled in bulk, about 1 hour. Lightly punch down, cover, and allow to rise for 30 minutes longer.

4. Shape the dough into a 13-inch loaf, being careful to press out any air. Grease a 13 x 4 x 4-inch Pullman or *pain de mie* bread pan (without the lid) and fit the loaf into the pan. Rub the top with butter, cover with plastic wrap, and let rise in a warm place for 2 hours.

5. Preheat the oven to 375°F.

6. Bake the loaf until golden brown and firm on top, about 30 minutes. Cool in the pan for 5 minutes; then unmold and let cool on a wire rack.

DEEP-DISH CHOCOLATE CREAM PIE

Chocolate cream pie has a place of honor in roadside diner pie cases across the country. This deconstructed version inverts the classic format because the gorgeous, silky, deeply chocolaty pudding is worth digging for. Break though a crunchy, buttery graham cracker crust and a smooth layer of whipped cream before making your way to the rich chocolate depths of this decadent "pie." Chocolate lovers, rejoice.

Serves 8

Chocolate Pudding

⅔ cup sugar

¼ cup unsweetened Dutch-processed cocoa powder

2 tablespoons cornstarch

½ teaspoon fine salt

3½ cups whole milk

3½ cups heavy cream

1 vanilla bean, split and seeds scraped, or 1½ teaspoons vanilla extract

1¼ pounds bittersweet chocolate (60% cacao), coarsely chopped

2 tablespoons unsalted butter

Graham Cracker Disks

½ pound (2 sticks) unsalted butter

½ vanilla bean, split and seeds scraped

2½ cups graham cracker crumbs (about 20 crackers)

1 cup sugar

Rum Whipped Cream

2 cups heavy cream, very cold

2 tablespoons confectioners' sugar

1 tablespoon dark rum (optional)

Seeds scraped from ½ vanilla bean or ½ teaspoon vanilla extract

1. To make the pudding, whisk together the sugar, cocoa, cornstarch, and salt in a medium heavy pan. Slowly whisk in the milk and cream and add the vanilla bean and seeds (if using).

2. Slowly bring the mixture to a boil over medium heat, whisking constantly. Once the mixture comes to a boil, let it boil for 1 minute. Remove the pan from the heat and whisk in the chocolate and butter, along with the vanilla extract, if using, until smooth. Strain the pudding through a fine-mesh sieve into a bowl and press a piece of plastic wrap directly onto the surface. Let cool at room temperature for 30 minutes; then transfer to the refrigerator and let chill completely, at least 4 hours and up to 24 hours.

3. To make the graham cracker disks, preheat the oven to 350°F.

4. Combine the butter and vanilla bean and seeds in a small saucepan and melt over low heat. Remove from the heat and keep warm. Discard the vanilla bean before using.

5. Combine the graham cracker crumbs and sugar in a medium bowl, add the melted butter, and stir until combined. Pat the mixture evenly and firmly into an 18 x 12-inch rimmed baking sheet. Bake until light golden brown and set, about 10 minutes. Let cool completely on a wire rack.

6. Using a 3-inch cookie cutter or a very sharp paring knife, carefully cut out 8 disks.

7. To make the whipped cream, combine the cream, sugar, rum, if using, and vanilla seeds in a large bowl and whip, using a handheld mixer or a balloon whisk, until soft peaks form.

8. Divide the pudding among 8 shallow bowls and spread some of the whipped cream evenly over the pudding. Top each with a graham cracker disk.

BLACKBERRY SOUFFLÉ

Nothing says "ta-da!" quite like a soufflé, making it a fitting finale for the most special of meals. With its dramatic presentation (the soufflé is delivered intact, then broken into and sauced tableside), this deep violet soufflé is one of the restaurant's most popular desserts. Colored and flavored with the essence of sweet and juicy blackberries, the texture of the delicate soufflé is light, airy—practically ethereal. The thick blackberry sauce, much like a crème anglaise, heightens the berry flavor and adds a wealth of richness to the dessert. Lemony whipped cream is the finishing touch.

Serves 6

4 tablespoons (½ stick) unsalted butter, plus more for the molds
⅓ cup plus 4 tablespoons sugar, plus more for the molds
1¼ cups frozen blackberries, thawed
1 tablespoon crème de cassis
¼ cup plus 2 teaspoons all-purpose flour
4 large egg yolks
5 large egg whites
Pinch of cream of tartar
Blackberry Sauce (recipe follows)
Lemon Whipped Cream (recipe follows)

1. Arrange a rack in the lower third of the oven and preheat the oven to 350°F. Generously butter six 8-ounce ramekins and coat with sugar, knocking out the excess. Set aside on a baking sheet.

2. Put ¾ cup of the blackberries in a food processor and process until smooth. Strain through a coarse-mesh strainer into a bowl and stir the cassis into the blackberry puree. Discard the seeds.

3. Combine 1¼ cups water, the remaining ½ cup blackberries, and 2 tablespoons of the sugar in a medium saucepan over medium heat and bring to a simmer. Cook until the sugar has melted and the berries are soft, about 5 minutes. Transfer the mixture to a food processor and process until smooth. Strain the blackberry juice through a coarse-mesh strainer, discarding the seeds, and keep warm.

4. Melt the 4 tablespoons butter in a small saucepan over medium-high heat. Whisk in the flour until smooth and cook for 1 minute. Whisk in the blackberry juice and cook, whisking constantly, until the mixture is thickened and pulls away from the sides of the pan. Transfer the mixture to a stand mixer fitted with the paddle attachment, add the blackberry puree, and beat until no more steam comes from the dough, about 2 minutes. Add the egg yolks, one at a time, and beat until smooth. Transfer to a large bowl and clean the mixer bowl.

5. Put the egg whites and cream of tartar in a stand mixer fitted with the whisk attachment and whip until frothy. Continue whipping, adding the remaining ⅓ cup plus 2 tablespoons sugar 1 tablespoon at a time, and whip until stiff peaks form. Gently fold the egg whites into the blackberry mixture until combined. (It is okay if a few streaks of the blackberry base are visible.)

6. Fill the prepared ramekins three-quarters full with the batter and bake on the baking sheet in the lower third of the oven until the soufflé rises and the tops are lightly browned, about 35 minutes. Remove from the oven. At the table, using a large spoon, break into the center of each soufflé and pour in some of the blackberry sauce. Top with a dollop of lemon whipped cream

BLACKBERRY SAUCE
Makes about 2 cups

1 cup whole milk
1 cup heavy cream
½ vanilla bean, split and seeds scraped
¼ cup good-quality blackberry preserves
4 large egg yolks
3 tablespoons sugar
2 teaspoons crème de cassis or crème de mûre

1. Bring the milk, heavy cream, vanilla bean and seeds, and blackberry preserves to a simmer in a small saucepan over medium heat.

2. Meanwhile, fill a large bowl halfway with ice water and have ready a smaller bowl that will fit inside it. Also have ready a fine-mesh strainer.

3. Whisk together the egg yolks and sugar in a medium bowl until pale. Slowly whisk in the warm milk mixture until combined. Remove the vanilla bean, return the mixture to the pan over medium heat, and cook, stirring constantly with a wooden spoon, until the mixture coats the back of the spoon, about 4 minutes. Stir in the crème de cassis.

4. Remove the sauce from the heat, immediately strain the mixture into the smaller bowl, and set in the ice bath to stop the cooking, stirring until the mixture is cool. Cover and refrigerate for at least 1 hour and up to 8 hours before serving.

LEMON WHIPPED CREAM
Makes 2 cups

1 cup heavy cream, very cold
1 teaspoon finely grated lemon zest
3 tablespoons confectioners' sugar
Seeds scraped from ½ vanilla bean or 1 teaspoon vanilla extract

Combine the heavy cream, lemon zest, confectioners' sugar, and vanilla seeds in a medium bowl and whip until soft peaks form. Cover and refrigerate. The cream can be made 30 minutes ahead of time. Whip lightly again if needed before serving.

BLUEBERRY LEMON CRÊPES
BROWN BUTTER SAUCE

Though French by definition, these delicate and lemony crêpes are an American tribute, boasting a sweet filling of tart, silky lemon curd and a juicy blueberry compote. The black currant–flavored crème de cassis contributes a sophisticated undercurrent of berry flavor to the compote and enhances its deep purple-blue color. Just as a stack of blueberry pancakes is made that much better by a melting pat of butter, a drizzle of browned butter enhances this dish with its nutty richness.

Serves 6

Lemon Curd
5 large egg yolks
¾ cup sugar
2 teaspoons finely grated lemon zest
⅓ cup fresh lemon juice
6 tablespoons (¾ stick) unsalted butter, cut into small pieces, chilled

Blueberry Compote
2 pints fresh or thawed frozen blueberries
½ cup sugar
1 teaspoon finely grated lemon zest
1 tablespoon fresh lemon juice
1 tablespoon cornstarch
2 tablespoons crème de cassis

Crêpes
2 large eggs
2 large egg yolks
2 tablespoons granulated sugar
1 tablespoon limoncello or 1 teaspoon finely grated lemon zest
1 cup whole milk
¾ cup all-purpose flour
3 tablespoons unsalted butter, melted and cooled slightly
Nonstick cooking spray
Brown Butter (page 200), warm
Confectioners' sugar
Chopped fresh mint leaves (optional), for garnish

1. To make the lemon curd, add enough water to a medium saucepan (or the bottom of a double boiler) to come about 1 inch up the side. Bring to a simmer over medium heat.

2. Put the egg yolks and sugar in a medium non-reactive metal bowl and whisk until smooth and pale yellow, about 1 minute. Add the lemon zest and juice and whisk until smooth.

3. Once the water reaches a simmer, reduce the heat under the pan to low and place the bowl with the egg mixture in it on top; the bowl should not touch the water. Cook, whisking constantly, until the curd thickens, is light yellow, and coats the back of a spoon, about 8 minutes.

4. Remove from the heat and whisk in the butter a piece at a time, allowing each addition to melt before adding the next. Transfer to a clean bowl and press a piece of plastic wrap directly on the surface of the curd. Refrigerate until cold, at least 2 hours or overnight.

5. To make the blueberry compote, combine 1 pint of the blueberries, the sugar, and the lemon zest and juice in a medium saucepan over high heat. Bring to a boil and cook until the sugar has melted and the berries are soft, 5 minutes.

6. Stir together the cornstarch and 1½ tablespoons water in a small bowl. Stir into the blueberries and cook until thickened, about 1 minute. Remove from the heat and add the crème de cassis and the remaining 1 pint blueberries. Let cool to room temperature. The compote can be covered and refrigerated for up to 1 day.

7. To make the crêpes, whisk together the eggs, yolks, and granulated sugar in a medium bowl until smooth. Add the limoncello and milk and mix until combined.

8. Add the flour and mix until just smooth. Stir in the butter. Cover the bowl and let sit for 30 minutes at room temperature or refrigerate for up to 4 hours.

(recipe continues)

9. Line a large plate with parchment or wax paper. Heat a crêpe pan or an 8-inch nonstick skillet over medium heat and spray with cooking spray. Add 3 tablespoons crêpe batter to the skillet and immediately tilt and swirl the skillet to spread the batter evenly over the bottom. Cook until the center of the crêpe is cooked through and the edges are lightly browned, about 1 minute. Gently flip and cook the other side for 20 seconds. Invert the crêpe onto the prepared plate. Repeat with the remaining batter, spraying the pan with cooking spray and placing parchment paper between crêpes. The crêpes can be made 1 day in advance, covered, and refrigerated.

10. Preheat the oven to 325°F. Line a baking sheet with parchment paper.

11. Place the crêpes, pale side up, on a flat surface and spread about 3 tablespoons of the lemon curd down the center of each crêpe. Using a slotted spoon, top the curd with some of the blueberry compote (reserve the leftover blueberry syrup), then roll up each crêpe. Arrange the crêpes, seam side down, on the baking sheet, brush the tops with a little of the brown butter, and sprinkle with a little confectioners' sugar. Heat in the oven until just warm, 1 to 2 minutes.

12. Drizzle some of the brown butter and blueberry compote syrup onto 6 large plates. Place 2 crêpes on each plate, drizzle the tops with a little more of the brown butter and some of the blueberry syrup, and garnish with mint if desired.

BROWN BUTTER
Makes about ½ cup

> 8 tablespoons (1 stick) unsalted butter, quartered
> Pinch of kosher salt

Combine the butter and salt in a medium sauté pan over medium-high heat and cook, swirling the pan several times, until golden brown, about 2 minutes. Serve hot.

GERMAN'S CHOCOLATE CAKE
COCONUT-PECAN-CAJETA FROSTING

German's Chocolate Cake is every bit as American as apple pie. *German* refers not to the country but rather to the last name of the originator of the type of chocolate used in the original recipe—Baker's German's Sweet Chocolate. I've kept the essentials of the classic recipe in place—chocolate cake layered with caramel, coconut, and pecans—but tweaked them just enough to proudly call this version my own. The cake itself is dark, moist, and truly chocolaty, and a glaze of chocolate ganache heightens the chocolate flavor without the overpowering sweetness of a traditional buttercream frosting. The real twist is found in the cake's inner layers: my caramel of choice is cajeta, a liquid dulce de leche Mexican treat of sweetened goat's milk cooked into a rich, syrupy caramel with smooth coconut milk. And forget a scoop of vanilla ice cream; fluffy coconut whipped cream is the last touch in this to-die-for dessert.

Makes 1 (9-inch) layer cake

Chocolate Cake
12 tablespoons (1½ sticks) unsalted butter, at room temperature, plus more for the pans
2¼ cups all-purpose flour
3 teaspoons baking powder
¾ teaspoon baking soda
¾ teaspoon fine salt
1 cup plus 2 tablespoons unsweetened Dutch-processed cocoa powder
1½ cups packed light muscovado sugar
1½ cups granulated sugar
1½ cups strong brewed black coffee, at room temperature
1½ cups buttermilk
3 large eggs
2 teaspoons vanilla extract

Frosting
1¾ cups whole milk
1¾ cups canned unsweetened coconut milk
1 cup goat's milk or additional whole milk
¾ cup plus 1 tablespoon sugar

Seeds scraped from ½ vanilla bean
2 tablespoons light corn syrup
2 tablespoons unsalted butter, cut into small pieces, chilled
½ teaspoon vanilla extract
⅛ teaspoon fine salt
2 teaspoons coconut rum (optional)
1¼ cups coarsely chopped pecans, toasted (see page 250)
1¼ cups sweetened shredded coconut

Ganache
1 cup heavy cream
8 ounces bittersweet chocolate, finely chopped
2 tablespoons light corn syrup

½ cup sweetened shredded coconut, toasted (see page 250), for garnish
Coconut Whipped Cream (page 203), for serving

1. To bake the cake, center a rack in the oven and preheat the oven to 325°F. Butter two 9-inch cake pans and line the bottoms with parchment paper.

2. Whisk together the flour, baking powder, baking soda, and salt in a medium bowl.

3. Melt the 12 tablespoons butter in a medium saucepan over medium heat. Whisk in the cocoa powder and cook for 1 minute. Remove from the heat, add the muscovado and granulated sugars, and whisk until the sugar is dissolved. Add the coffee, buttermilk, eggs, and vanilla and continue whisking until smooth. Add the dry ingredients and whisk until just combined.

4. Divide the batter evenly between the prepared cake pans and bake on the middle rack until a toothpick inserted into the center comes out with a few moist crumbs attached, 40 to 45 minutes. Let cool in the pans on a wire rack for 20 minutes. Then invert the cakes onto the wire rack and let cool for at least 1 hour before frosting.

(recipe continues)

5. To make the frosting, bring the milk, coconut milk, and goat's milk to a simmer in a small saucepan over low heat. Keep warm while you prepare the caramel.

6. Combine the sugar and ¼ cup water in a medium saucepan over high heat and cook without stirring until a deep amber brown color, 8 minutes. Slowly and carefully whisk in the warm milk mixture and continue whisking until smooth. Add the vanilla seeds and corn syrup. Bring to a boil, reduce the heat to medium, and cook, stirring occasionally with a wooden spoon, until the mixture is reduced by half and has the consistency of a caramel sauce, about 55 minutes.

7. Remove from the heat and whisk in the butter, vanilla, salt, and rum if using. Transfer the mixture to a medium bowl and stir in the pecans and shredded coconut. Let the frosting cool to room temperature, stirring occasionally, before frosting the cake.

8. Slice each cake layer in half horizontally. Place one cake layer on a cake round and spread one-third of the frosting evenly over the top. Repeat to make 3 layers and top with the remaining cake layer, top side up.

9. To make the ganache, bring the cream to a simmer. Put the chocolate in a medium bowl, add the hot cream and the corn syrup, and let sit for 30 seconds. Gently whisk until smooth. Let sit at room temperature for 10 minutes before pouring over the cake.

10. Set the cake on a wire rack set over a rimmed baking sheet. Pour the chocolate ganache over the cake, letting the excess drip off. Top with the toasted coconut. Let sit at room temperature for at least 30 minutes and up to 8 hours before slicing.

11. Slice the cake and top each slice with a dollop of the whipped cream.

COCONUT WHIPPED CREAM
Makes about 3½ cups

> 1½ cups heavy cream, very cold
> ¼ cup cream of coconut, such as Coco Lopez
> 2 tablespoons confectioners' or granulated sugar
> 1 teaspoon coconut rum
> ½ teaspoon vanilla extract

Combine the heavy cream, cream of coconut, sugar, rum, and vanilla in a mixer fitted with the whisk attachment and mix until soft peaks form.

RED VELVET CAKE

Once the Deep South's secret, red velvet cake definitely has the nation's attention. The cake's distinctive color, the result of a chemical reaction between acidic vinegar and buttermilk and Dutch-processed cocoa, was originally much more subdued than that of its present incarnation. A dose of food coloring is called for to pump that reddish brown into the true red that distinguishes this cake from all the rest. The sweet and lightly chocolaty cake is layered and frosted with an indulgently rich vanilla buttercream. Made with vanilla bean seeds instead of extract, the creamy frosting sports the telltale brown flecks that signal the pure vanilla flavor to come. Some red velvet cakes I've tried have been a bit on the dry side, but not this one. It's incredibly moist thanks to the buttermilk and a measure of canola oil.

Makes 1 (9-inch) layer cake

Cake
12 tablespoons (1½ sticks) unsalted butter, at room temperature, plus more for the pans
3¾ cups all-purpose flour, plus more for the pans
3 tablespoons unsweetened Dutch-processed cocoa powder
1½ teaspoons baking soda
½ teaspoon fine salt
2¼ cups sugar
¾ cup canola oil
3 large eggs, at room temperature
1½ teaspoons vanilla extract
1½ teaspoons red wine vinegar
1 tablespoon red food coloring
1½ cups buttermilk, at room temperature

Frosting
¼ cup heavy cream
1½ cups whole milk
½ vanilla bean, split and seeds scraped
¼ cup plus 3 tablespoons all-purpose flour
¾ pound (3 sticks) unsalted butter, softened
1½ cups superfine sugar

1. To make the cake, preheat the oven to 350°F. Butter and flour two 9-inch round cake pans and line the bottom of each pan with parchment paper.

2. Whisk together the flour, cocoa powder, baking soda, and salt in a small bowl.

3. Beat the butter, sugar, and oil in a stand mixer fitted with the paddle attachment until light and fluffy. Add the eggs, one at a time, scraping down the sides of the bowl, and beat until incorporated. Beat in the vanilla, vinegar, and food coloring.

4. Add the flour mixture to the batter in 3 batches, alternating with the buttermilk and mixing well after each addition. Divide the batter evenly between the prepared pans and bake for 30 to 40 minutes or until a wooden skewer inserted into the center comes out with a few moist crumbs attached. Cool on a wire rack for 15 minutes before removing the cakes from the pans. Let cool completely on the rack before frosting.

5. To make the frosting, combine the cream, milk, and vanilla bean and seeds in a small saucepan and bring to a simmer over medium-high heat. Remove the vanilla bean and discard. Add the flour and cook, whisking constantly, until thickened to a paste, about 2 minutes. Scrape into a bowl, cover, and refrigerate until very cold, at least 3 hours.

6. Combine the butter and sugar in a stand mixer fitted with the whisk attachment and beat until the mixture is very fluffy and the sugar is totally dissolved, about 6 minutes. Add the cold paste, a few tablespoons at a time, to the butter mixture and whip until light and fluffy.

7. Slice each cake layer in half horizontally. Place one cake layer on a cake round and spread about one-fifth of the frosting evenly over the top. Repeat to make 3 layers and top with the remaining cake layer, top side up. Use the remaining frosting to frost the top and sides of the cake. The cake will keep for up to 8 hours at cool room temperature.

8. To serve, slice the cake into pieces.

BOURBON PRALINE PROFITEROLES
BUTTERMILK ICE CREAM

OK, in my wildest dreams I couldn't come up with a more perfect dessert for myself. Bourbon, ice cream, buttermilk, pecans, and light, buttery-crispy profiteroles; it doesn't get any better for me (except for maybe the Blueberry Lemon Crêpes, page 198 . . . oh, and the Blackberry Soufflé, page 196). For some reason my sweet tooth always leans toward anything southern, and anything with bourbon in it is all right by me.

Makes 8 profiteroles with 1 quart ice cream; serves 4 or 8

Buttermilk Praline Ice Cream
1½ cups heavy cream
1 vanilla bean, split and seeds scraped
8 large egg yolks
½ cup sugar
1½ cups buttermilk
2 teaspoons vanilla extract
1 cup coarsely chopped store-bought pralines, plus more for garnish

Profiteroles
Nonstick cooking spray
6 tablespoons (¾ stick) unsalted butter
3 tablespoons sugar
¼ teaspoon fine salt
¾ cup all-purpose flour
3 large eggs
¼ cup whole milk
Bourbon Toffee Sauce (recipe follows)

1. To make the ice cream, prepare an ice bath by filling a large bowl with ice and water and nestling a medium bowl in the ice.

2. Bring the cream and vanilla bean and seeds to a simmer in a medium saucepan over medium heat.

3. Whisk together the yolks and sugar in a medium bowl until the mixture is pale and thick. Slowly whisk the warm cream into the yolk mixture. Remove the vanilla bean, return the entire mixture to the sauce-

pan, and cook, stirring constantly with a wooden spoon, until the mixture coats the back of the spoon, about 3 minutes. Strain the mixture into the bowl set inside the ice bath, add the buttermilk and vanilla, and stir until it is very cold, about 5 minutes.

4. Transfer the chilled mixture to an ice cream maker and freeze according to the manufacturer's instructions. Scrape the ice cream into a large bowl and fold in the pralines. Cover tightly and store in the freezer until firm, at least 4 hours.

5. To make the profiteroles, position a rack in the upper third of the oven and preheat the oven to 425°F. Line a large baking sheet with parchment paper and spray the parchment lightly with cooking spray.

6. Bring the butter, ¾ cup water, 1 tablespoon of the sugar, and the salt to a boil in a small heavy saucepan over high heat, stirring until the butter is melted. Reduce the heat to medium, add the flour all at once, and cook, beating with a wooden spoon, until the mixture pulls away from the side of the pan and forms a ball, about 30 seconds.

7. Transfer the mixture to the bowl of a stand mixer fitted with the paddle attachment and let cool slightly, about 5 minutes. Add the eggs one at a time, beating well after each addition, and mix until the mixture is smooth.

8. Scrape the mixture into a large pastry bag fitted with a ¾-inch plain tip and pipe eight disks (about 1½ inches in diameter and about ½ inch thick) onto the prepared baking sheet, spacing them at least 1½ inches apart. Brush the tops with the milk and sprinkle with the remaining 2 tablespoons sugar.

9. Bake the profiteroles for 15 minutes. Reduce the oven temperature to 400°F and continue to bake until the profiteroles are golden, puffed, and crisp, about 15 minutes. Turn off the oven. Remove the baking sheet from the oven, immediately pierce the side of each profiterole with the tip of a paring knife, and return to the oven to dry, propping the door slightly ajar, for 5 minutes. Halve a profiterole horizontally: If it is still moist inside, return the profiteroles to the oven and continue to dry with the door ajar for 5 minutes more. Cool the profiteroles completely on the baking sheet set on a wire rack, at least 25 minutes. The profiteroles can be made 1 day in advance. Store in a container with a tight-fitting lid. Crisp on a baking sheet in a preheated 350°F oven for a few minutes. Let cool before proceeding.

10. Spoon some of the sauce into the bottom of large shallow bowls. Halve the profiteroles horizontally and fill the bottoms with scoops of the ice cream; replace the tops. Spoon more sauce on top and garnish with chopped praline.

BOURBON TOFFEE SAUCE
Makes about 2 cups

2 cups heavy cream
½ cup sugar
½ cup dark corn syrup
¼ cup good-quality bourbon, such as Maker's Mark
1 teaspoon vanilla extract
2 tablespoons unsalted butter

1. Pour the cream into a small saucepan and bring to a simmer over low heat.

2. Combine the sugar and ¼ cup water in a medium saucepan over high heat and cook without stirring until a deep amber brown color, about 6 minutes. Add the corn syrup and bourbon and cook, stirring carefully, for 1 minute.

3. Slowly whisk in the warm cream (the mixture will bubble up) and whisk until smooth. Remove from the heat and whisk in the vanilla and butter. The sauce can be made 2 days in advance and stored covered in the refrigerator. Reheat slowly over low heat or in the microwave.

THIN APPLE TART
CINNAMON CRÈME ANGLAISE

The apple tart is France's answer to American apple pie. (Or maybe it's the other way around, but really, who's keeping score?) The light and buttery crust is a delicious home for overlapping slices of lightly seasoned apples. Rolling the dough over a bed of sugar fuses the granules to the crust, creating a sugary layer that caramelizes into a tantalizingly crisp outer shell as the tart bakes. I like to serve this with crème anglaise—a silky vanilla-infused pourable custard—flavored with apple's favorite spice, cinnamon. It adds just the right amount of richness to the elegant tart. A little ice cream on the side—vanilla or caramel, for example—wouldn't hurt either.

Serves 4 to 6

Tart Dough

¼ cup sour cream, chilled

1 large egg yolk

1¼ cups plus 2 tablespoons all-purpose flour

¼ teaspoon fine salt

8 tablespoons (1 stick) unsalted butter,
    cut into pieces, chilled

½ cup sugar

Apples

1½ cups apple juice

Juice of ½ lemon

¼ cup granulated sugar

1 tablespoon light brown sugar

¼ teaspoon ground cinnamon

1 to 2 Granny Smith apples, peeled, cored,
    and halved

Cinnamon Crème Anglaise (recipe follows),
    for serving

1. To make the tart dough, whisk together the sour cream and egg yolk in a small bowl.

2. Put the flour and salt in a food processor and pulse a few times to combine. Scatter the butter over the top of the flour and pulse 6 to 8 times, until the butter resembles coarse crumbs. Add the sour cream mixture and pulse until the dough just comes together. Scrape the dough onto a flat surface, flatten into a disk, wrap in plastic wrap, and refrigerate until the dough is cold, at least 1 hour and up to 2 weeks.

3. Spread the sugar over a flat surface. Place the disk of dough on the sugar and turn to coat in the sugar. Roll the dough out to a 14-inch circle that's ⅛ inch thick, flipping the dough once in the sugar during the rolling. Using a 12-inch plate as your guide, cut out the dough into a 12-inch round. Transfer the dough to a baking sheet lined with parchment paper and refrigerate for at least 20 minutes.

4. Preheat the oven to 375°F.

5. To prepare the apples, combine the apple juice, lemon juice, sugars, and cinnamon in a small saucepan and cook, whisking occasionally, over high heat until slightly thickened and reduced to ½ cup, about 5 minutes. Cover the glaze and keep warm.

6. Slice the apple halves crosswise into paper-thin (about 1/16-inch) slices. Arrange the slices, overlapping them slightly, on the pastry round. Brush the tops of the apples with some of the warm glaze. Transfer the baking sheet to the oven and bake the tart until the apples are soft and the pastry is golden brown, 35 to 40 minutes.

7. Remove from the oven and immediately brush the tops of the apples with more of the warm apple glaze. Using a large metal spatula, carefully transfer the tart to a wire rack and let cool for 10 minutes before serving.

8. Ladle some of the cinnamon crème anglaise onto large dinner plates and top with a slice of the apple tart.

CINNAMON CRÈME ANGLAISE
Makes about 2 cups

1 cup whole milk
1 cup heavy cream
½ teaspoon ground cinnamon
1 cinnamon stick
½ vanilla bean, split and seeds scraped
6 large egg yolks
½ cup sugar

1. Prepare an ice bath by placing a medium bowl inside a larger bowl filled half full with ice water.

2. Put the milk, cream, cinnamon, cinnamon stick, and vanilla bean and seeds in a medium saucepan and bring to a simmer over low heat. Remove from the heat.

3. Whisk together the egg yolks and sugar in a medium bowl. Gradually whisk in the hot milk mixture. Remove the cinnamon stick and vanilla bean, and return the entire mixture to the saucepan. Cook, stirring constantly with a wooden spoon, over medium-low heat until the custard thickens and leaves a path on the back of the spoon when you draw your finger across, about 2 minutes.

4. Strain the custard into the bowl set in the ice bath and stir until chilled. Cover and refrigerate until cold, 3 hours or overnight.

SWEET POTATO PIE
CINNAMON CRUNCH ICE CREAM

Sweet potato pie is as southern as desserts come. Though it is a favorite in the soul food repertoire, you do not often see it on tables north of the Mason–Dixon line and west of the Mississippi. A traditional ending to Thanksgiving dinner, this silken pie is due for a nation-wide comeback as a delicious finale to any fall or winter meal. I love to see an ingredient cross the preconceived boundaries of savory and sweet, and the naturally high sugar content in the potatoes makes its shift from dinner to dessert a seamless one. Yes, you could serve it with store-bought vanilla ice cream, but time dedicated to making your own rich ice cream studded with buttery clusters of cinnamon-spiced graham cracker crumbles is time well spent. Everyone at your table—Thanksgiving or anytime—will be glad you did.

Makes 1 (9-inch) pie

Sweet Potato Filling
2 pounds sweet potatoes
3 large eggs
½ cup granulated sugar
¼ cup packed light brown sugar
2 tablespoons molasses
2 teaspoons ground cinnamon
¼ teaspoon fine salt
1 teaspoon vanilla extract
1¼ cups evaporated milk
2 tablespoons unsalted butter,
     melted and cooled

Graham Cracker Crust
2 cups graham cracker crumbs (about
     15 crackers)
8 tablespoons (1 stick) unsalted butter, melted
⅛ teaspoon ground cinnamon
2 large egg yolks, whisked with 2 teaspoons
     water

Cinnamon Crunch Ice Cream (recipe follows)

1. Preheat the oven to 375°F.

2. Prick the sweet potatoes several times with a fork, place on a baking sheet, and roast in the oven until soft, about 45 minutes. Remove from the oven and let cool slightly. When cool enough to handle, halve each potato lengthwise and use a small spoon to scrape the flesh into a medium bowl; discard the skins. While the potatoes are still hot, mash with a potato masher or fork until slightly smooth.

3. To make the crust, reduce the oven temperature to 350°F. Combine the graham cracker crumbs, butter, and cinnamon in a bowl and mix until combined. Evenly press the crumbs into a deep-dish 9-inch pie plate and brush with the egg yolk mixture. Bake until light golden brown and firm, about 12 minutes. Remove from the oven and let cool on a wire rack. Keep the oven on.

4. To make the filling, whisk together the eggs, sugars, molasses, cinnamon, and salt in a medium bowl. Whisk in the vanilla and milk. Gradually add the egg mixture to the sweet potatoes, whisking gently to combine. Add the butter and whisk until incorporated.

5. Place the pie shell on a baking sheet and pour the sweet potato mixture into the shell. Bake until the filling is set around edges but the center jiggles slightly when shaken, about 45 minutes. Transfer the pie to a wire rack and let cool to room temperature, about 2 hours. Serve at room temperature or refrigerate until chilled, about 2 hours and up to 12 hours.

6. Slice the pie into pieces and serve each one with a large scoop of the ice cream.

CINNAMON CRUNCH ICE CREAM
Makes 1 quart

¼ cup all-purpose flour

¼ cup quick-cooking rolled oats

¼ cup plus 2 tablespoons packed light
   brown sugar

2¼ teaspoons ground cinnamon

4 tablespoons (½ stick) unsalted butter,
   cut into pieces, chilled

2 cups whole milk

2 cups heavy cream

2 cinnamon sticks

1 vanilla bean, split and seeds scraped

8 large egg yolks

1 cup granulated sugar

1. Preheat the oven to 350°F. Line a baking sheet with parchment paper.

2. Combine the flour, oats, brown sugar, and ground cinnamon in a food processor and process a few times to combine. Add the butter and pulse until combined. Pat the mixture evenly into a 4-inch square on the baking sheet. Bake until golden brown and crispy, about 15 minutes. Remove and let cool. Chop the cinnamon crunch into small pieces and set aside.

3. Combine the milk, heavy cream, cinnamon sticks, and vanilla bean and seeds in a medium saucepan and bring to a simmer over medium heat. Remove and let steep for 30 minutes. Return to the heat and bring to a simmer.

4. Prepare an ice bath by placing a medium bowl inside a larger bowl filled half full with ice water. Whisk together the yolks and granulated sugar until pale yellow. Slowly whisk in the warm milk mixture. Remove the cinnamon sticks and vanilla bean, return the mixture to the pan, and cook, stirring with a wooden spoon, until the mixture coats the back of the spoon, 3 to 4 minutes. Strain the custard into the bowl set in the ice bath and stir until chilled.

5. Pour the custard into an ice cream maker and freeze according to the manufacturer's directions. Fold the cinnamon crunch into the soft ice cream, cover, and freeze until hardened, at least 2 hours.

PUMPKIN BREAD PUDDING
SPICY CARAMEL APPLE SAUCE

This fantastic dessert is perfect for the cool months of late fall and winter. Cubes of tender pumpkin bread are baked in a rich custard laced with bourbon and maple syrup. Crisp apple cider is the base of a buttery caramel sauce spiced with fresh ginger, cinnamon, nutmeg, and star anise. Forget about serving the same-old pumpkin pie at Thanksgiving and put this out instead for a new twist on two old classics. The recipe includes directions for making your own pumpkin bread to use in the pudding, but you can of course also use a loaf of pumpkin bread from your favorite bakery. Brioche or cinnamon-raisin bread would also work perfectly.

Serves 8

Unsalted butter, for the pan
8 cups ½-inch cubed Pumpkin Bread
    (page 214) or other bread
2 cups heavy cream
1 cup whole milk
1 vanilla bean, split and seeds scraped
6 large egg yolks
½ cup sugar
3 tablespoons pure maple syrup
1 cup canned pumpkin puree, *not* flavored
    pie filling
2 tablespoons bourbon
Freshly whipped cream, for serving
Spicy Caramel Apple Sauce (page 214)
Shelled pumpkin seeds (optional), for garnish

1. Preheat the oven to 325°F. Butter a 10-inch glass baking dish.

2. Spread the bread cubes on a large baking sheet and bake in the oven, turning once, until lightly toasted, about 15 minutes. Let cool.

3. Combine the cream, milk, and vanilla bean and seeds in a small saucepan over medium heat and bring to a simmer.

4. Whisk together the yolks, sugar, maple syrup, and pumpkin puree in a large bowl. Slowly whisk in the hot cream mixture until combined. Discard the vanilla bean and whisk in the bourbon.

5. Scatter the pumpkin bread cubes in the prepared baking dish. Pour the custard over the bread, pressing down on the bread to totally submerge it in the custard. Let sit for 15 minutes to allow the bread to soak up some of the custard.

6. Place the dish in a larger roasting pan and pour hot water into the roasting pan until it comes halfway up the sides of the glass dish. Bake until the sides are slightly puffed and the center jiggles slightly, about 1 hour. Remove from the oven and the water bath and cool on a wire rack for at least 30 minutes before serving.

7. Serve the warm bread pudding topped with whipped cream and drizzled with spicy caramel apple sauce. Sprinkle with pumpkin seeds if desired.

(recipe continues)

PUMPKIN BREAD
Makes 1 (9-inch) loaf

4 tablespoons unsalted butter, softened,
    plus more for the pan

1¾ cups all-purpose flour

½ teaspoon fine salt

1 teaspoon baking soda

½ teaspoon baking powder

1 teaspoon ground cinnamon

½ teaspoon freshly grated nutmeg

¼ teaspoon ground allspice

¼ teaspoon ground cloves

1½ cups sugar

¼ cup vegetable oil

Scant 1 cup canned pumpkin puree,
    not flavored pie filling

2 large eggs

1. Preheat the oven to 350°F. Butter a 9-inch loaf pan.

2. Whisk together the flour, salt, baking soda, baking powder, cinnamon, nutmeg, allspice, and cloves in a small bowl.

3. Beat the butter, sugar, and oil on high speed in the bowl of a stand mixer fitted with the paddle attachment, scraping down the sides and bottom of the bowl a few times, until light and fluffy, about 1 minute.

4. Add the pumpkin puree and mix until combined. Add the eggs, one at a time, and mix until just incorporated. Mixing on low speed, slowly add the flour mixture and ⅔ cup water and mix until just combined. Spread the batter into the prepared pan and bake until a toothpick inserted into the center comes out clean, 1 hour to 1 hour 15 minutes. Let cool in the pan on a wire rack for 10 minutes. Remove from the pan and let cool completely.

SPICY CARAMEL APPLE SAUCE
Makes about 2 cups

1 cup heavy cream

½ cup apple juice

1 star anise

1 (1-inch) piece fresh ginger, peeled and chopped

4 cloves

2 cinnamon sticks

⅛ teaspoon freshly grated nutmeg

1½ cups sugar

1 tablespoon apple cider vinegar

1 tablespoon apple schnapps

1. Combine the cream, apple juice, star anise, ginger, cloves, cinnamon sticks, and nutmeg in a small saucepan and bring to a simmer. Remove from the heat and let steep for at least 20 minutes. Strain the mixture into a clean small saucepan and place back over low heat while you make the caramel.

2. Combine the sugar, ½ cup water, and the vinegar in a medium saucepan over high heat and cook without stirring until a deep amber color, 8 to 10 minutes. Slowly and carefully whisk in the warm cream mixture a little at a time, and continue whisking until smooth. Add the apple schnapps and cook for 30 seconds longer. Transfer to a bowl and keep warm. The sauce can be made 2 days in advance and refrigerated. Reheat over low heat before serving.

PISTACHIO CRÈME CARAMEL
RASPBERRY WHIPPED CREAM

This make-ahead dessert is a great choice for dinner parties—the individual servings take very little time to plate and garnish, so you can enjoy yourself while still wowing your dinner guests with an elegant, delicious finale. The recipe's first step calls for infusing its liquid ingredients with chopped pistachios; though the nuts themselves are later strained and removed, their fresh, delicate sweetness flavors every creamy spoonful of the rich custard. Prepared pistachio paste (available online; see Sources) adds more nuttiness and body.

Serves 6

1½ cups heavy cream
1½ cups whole milk
1 cup unsalted pistachios, chopped
1½ cups sugar
2 tablespoons pistachio paste
3 large egg yolks
2 large eggs
⅛ teaspoon fine salt
1 tablespoon amaretto or ¼ teaspoon almond extract
Raspberry Whipped Cream (recipe follows)
Fresh raspberries, for garnish
Fresh mint sprigs, for garnish

1. Combine the cream and milk in a medium saucepan and bring to a simmer over medium heat. Stir in the pistachios, remove from the heat, cover, and refrigerate for at least 4 hours and up to 24 hours.

2. Put six 8-ounce ramekins in a roasting pan.

3. Put 1 cup of the sugar and ½ cup water in a small saucepan and bring to a boil over moderately high heat, stirring until the sugar is dissolved. Boil without stirring until the syrup begins to turn a light golden brown, about 5 minutes. Continue to boil, swirling the pan occasionally, until the syrup is a deep amber color. Immediately divide the caramel among the ramekins, tilting if necessary to coat the bottoms.

4. Put a rack in the center of the oven and preheat the oven to 325°F.

5. Add ¼ cup of the remaining sugar and the pistachio paste to the cream mixture and bring to a simmer over medium heat. Whisk together the yolks, eggs, salt, and remaining ¼ cup sugar in a medium bowl until pale. Slowly whisk the warm cream mixture into the eggs and whisk until combined. Whisk in the amaretto. Strain the mixture into a large bowl and then ladle the custard into the prepared ramekins, filling each one three-quarters full.

6. Carefully add enough warm water to the roasting pan to reach halfway up the sides of the ramekins. Bake in the middle of the oven until the custard is just set but still trembles slightly in the center, 40 to 50 minutes. Transfer the ramekins to a wire rack and cool at room temperature for 30 minutes. Chill, loosely covered, for at least 2 hours and up to 24 hours.

7. To unmold, invert a plate over each ramekin and invert the custard onto the plate. (The custards can also be served in their molds.) Top with raspberry whipped cream and garnish with fresh raspberries and mint sprigs.

RASPBERRY WHIPPED CREAM
Makes about 2½ cups

1 cup fresh raspberries
2 tablespoons granulated sugar
1 cup heavy cream, very cold
2 tablespoons confectioners' sugar
2 teaspoons amaretto or ⅛ teaspoon almond extract
½ teaspoon vanilla extract

1. Combine the raspberries and granulated sugar in a small saucepan and cook over medium-high heat until the sugar is melted, the raspberries are soft, and the mixture is thickened, about 8 minutes. Remove from the heat and let cool completely.

2. Combine the cream, confectioners' sugar, amaretto, and vanilla in a large bowl and whip until stiff peaks form. Gently fold in the raspberry mixture.

BRUNCH

BLUE CORN FRIED EGGS
RED AND GREEN CHILE SAUCES, BLACK BEANS

A Mexican-inspired brunch is my favorite way to recover from a long night out, and this spin on huevos rancheros is how we serve it up at Bar Americain. This plate is layered with taste and texture, from the crisp, salty tortillas up to the cool and chunky guacamole on top. Savory black beans make this dish extra satisfying, while the chile sauces pump up the color—and heat. I like the slightly sweet, nutty flavor of blue corn tortillas, but if you can't find them, yellow ones are an easy substitute.
Serves 4

Black Beans
1 cup dried black beans or 1 (16-ounce) can black
  beans, drained, rinsed, and drained again
½ small red onion, finely diced
2 cloves garlic, finely chopped
1 canned chipotle chile in adobo, finely chopped
½ teaspoon ground cumin
Kosher salt and freshly ground black pepper

Fried Blue Corn Tortillas
2 cups canola oil
8 (4-inch) corn tortillas, preferably blue
Kosher salt

Eggs
4 tablespoons (½ stick) unsalted butter
8 large eggs
Kosher salt and freshly ground black pepper

Red Chile Sauce (page 239)
Guacamole (recipe follows)
3 ounces queso fresco cheese, crumbled (¾ cup)
Green Chile Sauce (page 238)
¼ cup chopped fresh cilantro

1. If using dried beans, pick over the beans and discard any stones. Put in a bowl, cover generously with cold water, and let soak for at least 8 hours.

2. Drain the beans, put in a medium saucepan, and add cold water to cover by 2 inches. Add the onion, garlic, chipotle, and cumin and bring to a boil over high heat. Reduce the heat and simmer, adding more water if the beans appear dry, until the beans are tender, 1 to 1½ hours. Season with salt and pepper. The beans can be made 8 hours in advance and refrigerated. Reheat before serving.

3. If using canned beans, put them in a saucepan with the onion, garlic, chipotle, cumin, and 1 cup cold water and bring to a boil over medium heat. Cook for 5 minutes. Season with salt and pepper.

4. To fry the tortillas, heat the oil in a medium saucepan over medium heat until it reaches 350°F on a deep-fat thermometer. Fry the tortillas, one at a time, turning once, until just crispy, 20 to 30 seconds. Transfer to a plate lined with paper towels and season lightly with salt.

5. To cook the eggs, melt the butter in large nonstick sauté pan over medium heat. Carefully crack the eggs into the pan, season with salt and pepper, and cook until the whites are completely firm but the yolks are still soft, about 2 minutes.

6. To serve, put some of the red chile sauce in the center of 4 large plates and swirl to cover the bottom. Put 2 fried tortillas on each plate. Top each tortilla with a fried egg and top each egg with some of the guacamole and cheese. Drain the beans and spoon them along with some green chile sauce on the tortillas. Garnish with the chopped cilantro.

GUACAMOLE
Makes about 2 cups

2 ripe Hass avocados, peeled, pitted, and diced
½ small red onion, finely diced
1 jalapeño chile, finely diced
Juice of 1 lime
¼ cup chopped fresh cilantro
Kosher salt and freshly ground black pepper

Combine the avocado, onion, jalapeño, lime juice, and cilantro in a medium bowl and season with salt and pepper.

POACHED EGGS
TASSO HAM, GRIDDLED TOMATO, CAJUN HOLLANDAISE

Eggs Benedict is the quintessential dish of the New York Sunday brunch. I like to put a southern spin on the classic, starting with a fluffy buttermilk biscuit. A Cajun blend of seasonings gives a kick to the luscious hollandaise sauce, which is right at home with New Orleans' beloved tasso ham. Tasso is cured and hot-smoked pork shoulder crusted with a spicy blend of flavorings such as garlic and cayenne pepper. (If you can't find tasso, you can try substituting slices of Italian capicola, which is prepared similarly.) Griddled tomatoes are an addition to, not a substitution in, the original Benedict, but I like the slightly sweet, fresh balance they bring to the richness of the other components.
Serves 4

1 tablespoon white wine vinegar
4 large eggs
Kosher salt and freshly ground black pepper
2 tablespoons canola oil
½ pound tasso ham, sliced ¼ inch thick
4 plum tomatoes, sliced in half lengthwise
4 Black Pepper Buttermilk Biscuits (page 191)
Cajun Hollandaise (recipe follows)
Fresh flat-leaf parsley leaves, for garnish

1. Heat 3 cups water with the vinegar in a large deep skillet over medium heat until simmering. Break each egg into a cup and then gently add to the water. Poach for 4 to 5 minutes, or until the yolk is almost set. Remove the eggs from the pan with a slotted spoon to drain the liquid and place on a plate. Season with salt and pepper.

2. Heat the oil on a cast-iron griddle or pan until it begins to shimmer. Cook the ham until light golden brown, about 1 minute per side. Transfer to a plate lined with paper towels.

3. Cook the tomatoes on the hot griddle until light golden brown and just warmed through, about 20 seconds per side.

4. Split the biscuits horizontally. Place the bottoms on 4 large plates. Top each bottom with an egg. Drizzle with some of the hollandaise, top with ham, and sprinkle with parsley. Place the tomato halves and biscuit tops on the side.

CAJUN HOLLANDAISE
Makes about 1 cup

1½ teaspoons smoked sweet Spanish paprika
½ teaspoon ground New Mexico chile
Pinch of ground chile de árbol
Pinch of cayenne
¼ teaspoon garlic powder
¼ teaspoon onion powder
¼ teaspoon dried thyme
¼ teaspoon dried oregano
3 large egg yolks, lightly beaten
1 tablespoon fresh lemon juice
12 tablespoons (1½ sticks) unsalted butter, melted until foamy
1 teaspoon kosher salt
¼ teaspoon freshly ground black pepper

1. Stir together the paprika, New Mexico chile, chile de árbol, cayenne, garlic and onion powders, the thyme, and the oregano in a small bowl.

2. Bring 1 inch of water to a simmer in a medium saucepan (or in the bottom of a double boiler). Whisk together the egg yolks and lemon juice in a medium nonreactive metal bowl and set over the simmering water. Whisk the yolks until pale yellow and fluffy, about 4 minutes.

3. Slowly add the melted butter, a few tablespoons at a time, and whisk until thickened. Season the sauce with 2 teaspoons of the spice mixture, the salt, and the pepper. Serve warm.

MISS STEPHANIE'S BISCUITS
CREAM GRAVY, SAUSAGE, SCRAMBLED EGGS

My beautiful wife, Stephanie, may live in New York, but when it comes time for breakfast, she is still a Texas girl through and through. She can put away a plate of biscuits, sausage, and cream gravy like nobody's business. This dish was created in her honor. I highly recommend making your own sausage patties; it's so easy to do, and it puts you in total control of what you are eating. Think fresh herbs and garlic as opposed to the nitrates and excessive sodium you'll find in many supermarket sausages. A healthy dose of black pepper punches up the flavor of the silky cream gravy.

Serves 4

1 pound ground pork
2 cloves garlic, smashed and chopped to a paste
1 teaspoon onion powder
2 tablespoons finely chopped fresh sage
1 tablespoon finely chopped fresh thyme
2 tablespoons canola oil
Kosher salt and freshly ground black pepper
8 large eggs, lightly beaten
6 tablespoons (¾ stick) unsalted butter
8 Black Pepper Buttermilk Biscuits (page 191)
Cream Gravy (recipe follows)
Chopped fresh flat-leaf parsley leaves, for garnish

1. Combine the pork, garlic, onion powder, sage, thyme, and oil in a large bowl and season with salt and pepper. Cover and refrigerate for at least 30 minutes and up to 8 hours to allow the flavors to meld.

2. Form the sausage mixture into 8 patties, each ½ inch thick. Heat a large nonstick pan over high heat and cook the patties until golden brown on both sides and just cooked through, about 5 minutes per side.

3. Beat the eggs in a large bowl and season with salt and pepper. Melt the butter over low heat in a large nonstick skillet. Add the eggs and cook slowly, stirring constantly with a wooden spoon, until soft curds form.

4. Slice each biscuit in half, put a sausage patty on the bottom of each biscuit, and top with cream gravy and some parsley. Serve 2 biscuits per person, with the eggs and biscuit tops on the side.

CREAM GRAVY
Makes about 2 cups

2 cups whole milk
2 tablespoons unsalted butter
2 tablespoons all-purpose flour
1 teaspoon kosher salt
¼ teaspoon freshly ground black pepper

1. Put the milk in a small saucepan and bring to a simmer over medium heat.

2. Melt the butter in a small saucepan over medium heat. Whisk in the flour and cook for 1 minute without browning. Slowly whisk in the warm milk. Raise the heat to high and continue whisking until the sauce begins to thicken and the raw taste of the flour has been cooked out, about 5 minutes. Season with the salt and pepper. Serve warm.

OPEN-FACED FRIED EGG SANDWICHES

This is an egg sandwich I could eat for breakfast, lunch, and dinner. Tangy sourdough bread is grilled to crusty perfection and topped with a meaty slice of griddled country ham, blistered sweet tomatoes, and a perfectly fried egg. A lightly dressed mound of slightly bitter, feathery frisée crowns this fork-and-knife sandwich.

Serves 4

Frisée Salad

3 tablespoons white wine vinegar

2 teaspoons mayonnaise

1 teaspoon Dijon mustard

1 teaspoon whole grain mustard

Kosher salt and freshly ground black pepper

¼ cup extra virgin olive oil

2 cups chopped frisée

Sandwich

4 tablespoons (½ stick) unsalted butter

4 large eggs

Kosher salt and freshly ground black pepper

1 tablespoon canola oil

¼ pound country ham, sliced paper-thin

4 (¼-inch-thick) slices sourdough bread

¼ cup extra virgin olive oil

4 plum tomatoes, sliced in half lengthwise

1. To make the salad dressing, whisk together the vinegar, mayonnaise, and mustards in a medium bowl and season with salt and pepper. Slowly whisk in the olive oil until emulsified.

2. For the sandwich, melt the butter in a large nonstick sauté pan over medium heat and carefully crack the eggs into the pan. Season with salt and pepper and cook until the whites are completely firm, about 2 minutes. Carefully flip the eggs over and cook for 30 seconds longer.

3. Heat the canola oil on a cast-iron griddle or pan until it begins to shimmer. Cook the ham until light golden brown, about 1 minute per side. Transfer to a plate lined with paper towels.

4. Toast the bread on the hot griddle until light golden brown, about 30 seconds per side. Remove from the griddle and brush the top sides with the olive oil and season with salt and pepper.

5. Cook the tomatoes on the hot griddle until light golden brown and just warmed through, about 20 seconds per side.

6. Top the bread slices with a few slices of the ham, an egg, and 2 tomato halves. Toss the frisée in the dressing, season with salt and pepper, and place on top.

STEEL-CUT OATMEAL
APPLES, RAISINS, BURNT ORANGE CRUST, CINNAMON CREAM

Bland and mushy are forever banished; this is oatmeal for grown-ups. Steel-cut oatmeal (also referred to as *Irish oatmeal*) has a wonderfully nutty taste and a texture that is at once creamy and chewy. As a kid I always loaded my oatmeal with raisins and brown sugar; now I cook tart apple slices with the same ingredients for an unexpected yet familiar treat to layer with the oatmeal. A sprinkling of turbinado sugar and a quick hit from the broiler create a sweet brûléed crust and an extra touch of decadence. Crack the crust with your spoon and pour in the cinnamon-scented cream . . . oh yeah, you'll be in love with oatmeal after this.

Serves 4

Oatmeal
1¼ cups steel-cut oats
Pinch of kosher salt
2 teaspoons finely grated orange zest
½ cup whole milk
¼ cup packed light brown sugar

Topping
2 tablespoons granulated sugar
2 tablespoons pure maple syrup
⅛ teaspoon ground cinnamon
½ cup raisins
2 tablespoons unsalted butter
2 tablespoons light brown sugar
Pinch of fine salt
2 Granny Smith apples, peeled, cored, and cut into medium dice
4 tablespoons turbinado sugar (such as Sugar in the Raw)
Cinnamon Cream (recipe follows)

1. To cook the oatmeal, bring 5½ cups water to a boil in a medium saucepan over high heat. Stir in the oats, salt, and zest and bring to a boil. Reduce the heat to medium and continue cooking, stirring occasionally and adding more water if needed, until the oats are tender, 30 to 40 minutes. Stir in the milk and brown sugar and cook for 1 minute.

2. While the oatmeal is cooking, make the topping. Combine the granulated sugar, ¾ cup water, the maple syrup, and the cinnamon in a small saucepan and bring to a boil over high heat. Cook until the sugar is completely dissolved, about 1 minute. Remove from the heat, stir in the raisins, and let sit at room temperature for at least 20 minutes.

3. Heat the butter in a medium sauté pan over medium heat, add the brown sugar and salt, and cook until melted. Add the apples and the raisin mixture and cook, stirring occasionally, until the apples are soft, about 15 minutes.

4. Preheat the broiler.

5. Place a few tablespoons of the apple mixture in the bottom of 4 ovenproof bowls or ramekins. Divide half of the oatmeal on top. Make a second layer with the remaining apple mixture and top with the remaining oatmeal, smoothing out the top. Sprinkle 1 tablespoon of the turbinado sugar evenly over the top of each serving.

6. Place the bowls on a baking sheet and put under the broiler. Broil until the sugar is golden brown and completely melted, about 1 minute. Remove from the oven and let rest for a few minutes before serving. Crack the top of the sugar crust with a spoon and pour in some of the cinnamon cream. Serve immediately.

CINNAMON CREAM
Makes 1 scant cup

½ cup heavy cream
2 tablespoons crème fraîche or sour cream
2 tablespoons pure maple syrup
2 tablespoons fresh orange juice
½ teaspoon ground cinnamon

Whisk together the cream, crème fraîche, maple syrup, orange juice, and cinnamon in a small bowl.

CRACKED WHEAT WAFFLES
CINNAMON-ALLSPICE BUTTER, BLUEBERRY SYRUP

Nutty cracked wheat (okay, it's technically bulgur) adds a welcome touch of texture to these waffles. Made with whole wheat flour, the waffles are a bit healthier and heartier than standard ones without being the least bit leaden. Spicy cinnamon and complex allspice lend their flavors to the creamy butter. A sweet blueberry syrup drizzled—or ladled—over the waffles makes the whole dish special. I wouldn't recommend making the syrup with frozen berries as they are too wet to burst as the fresh berries do. If you have extra berries left over, sprinkle them on top before serving.

Serves 4 to 6

1 cup all-purpose flour
1 cup whole wheat flour
2 tablespoons sugar
2 teaspoons baking powder
1 teaspoon baking soda
1 teaspoon ground cinnamon
¼ teaspoon fine salt
2¼ cups buttermilk
2 large eggs
4 tablespoons (½ stick) unsalted butter, melted and cooled
2 tablespoons canola oil, plus more for cooking
½ cup fine bulgur
Cinnamon-Allspice Butter (recipe follows)
Blueberry Syrup (recipe follows)

1. Whisk together the flours, sugar, baking powder, baking soda, cinnamon, and salt in a large bowl.

2. Whisk together the buttermilk, eggs, butter, and oil in a separate large bowl. Add the flour mixture and bulgur to the buttermilk mixture and whisk until just combined. Let the batter rest for 15 minutes.

3. Preheat the oven to 200°F.

4. Heat a waffle iron according to the manufacturer's instructions and brush or spray with a little canola oil. Add the batter and cook until the waffles are golden brown, 3 to 4 minutes. Place on a baking sheet and keep warm in the oven while you cook the remaining waffles.

5. Top each waffle with some of the spiced butter and drizzle with the blueberry syrup.

CINNAMON-ALLSPICE BUTTER
Makes ½ cup

8 tablespoons (1 stick) unsalted butter, slightly softened
1 tablespoon honey
¼ teaspoon ground cinnamon
¼ teaspoon ground allspice
Pinch of fine salt

Stir together the butter, honey, cinnamon, allspice, and salt in a small bowl until combined. Cover and refrigerate for at least 30 minutes and up to 2 days before serving. Let soften slightly before serving.

BLUEBERRY SYRUP
Makes about 1 ¾ cups

1 cup pure maple syrup
¾ cup fresh blueberries

Combine the maple syrup and blueberries in a small saucepan and bring to simmer over medium heat. Cook until the blueberries soften slightly and the mixture is warm, about 5 minutes. Serve warm.

BUTTERMILK FLAPJACKS
ROASTED APRICOTS, PECANS, MAPLE SYRUP

It used to be that flapjacks were made from a corn-based batter, this being the major distinction between them and their close cousin pancakes, which were made from a wheat flour-based batter. Today the two terms are roughly synonymous, though I love the heartiness that the term *flapjacks* implies, and the three that we stack up per serving are more than enough to satisfy even the hungriest Bar Americain bruncher. That said, the buttermilk in the batter makes the flapjacks light and fluffy, as does taking care not to overmix the batter and giving it ample resting time before you start cooking. Instead of folding the tasty extras into the flapjack batter, I load warm maple syrup with the good stuff—crunchy pecans and sweet apricots. Apricot season is short, and finding really flavorful ones is not always easy, so I use dried apricots in the syrup, rehydrating them in simple syrup and then roasting them. The sugars are slightly caramelized in the process, and the fruit's sweet, slightly tart flavor is magnified.

Serves 4

1½ cups all purpose flour
3 tablespoons granulated sugar
1 teaspoon baking powder
½ teaspoon baking soda
¾ teaspoon fine salt
1½ cups buttermilk
3 tablespoons unsalted butter, melted
2 large eggs
½ teaspoon pure vanilla extract
Nonstick cooking spray
Roasted Apricot-Pecan Syrup (recipe follows)
Confectioners' sugar

1. Whisk together the flour, granulated sugar, baking powder, baking soda, and salt in a large bowl.

2. Whisk together the buttermilk, butter, eggs, and vanilla in a medium bowl. Add to the flour mixture and whisk until just combined; there should be a few lumps. Cover and refrigerate the batter for at least 30 minutes or for up to 1 hour.

3. Preheat the oven to 200°F.

4. Heat a griddle or large nonstick sauté pan over medium heat and spray with nonstick cooking spray. Ladle a scant ¼ cup of the batter onto the griddle for each flapjack. Cook until the bottom is lightly golden brown and bubbles form on the top of the cake, 2 to 3 minutes. Gently flip over and continue cooking for 30 to 45 seconds. Transfer to a platter and keep warm in the oven while you cook the remaining flapjacks.

5. Serve the flapjacks with some of the warm apricot syrup ladled over them. Sprinkle with confectioners' sugar.

ROASTED APRICOT-PECAN SYRUP
Makes about 2 cups

½ cup sugar
8 dried apricots
1 cup pure maple syrup
⅛ teaspoon ground cinnamon
½ cup pecans, toasted (page 250) and coarsely chopped

1. Combine 1 cup water and the sugar in a small saucepan and bring to a boil over high heat. Cook until the sugar is completely melted, 2 minutes. Remove from the heat, add the apricots, and let sit at room temperature for at least 30 minutes.

2. Preheat the oven to 350°F. Line a baking sheet with parchment paper.

3. Remove the apricots from the syrup with a slotted spoon and place in a single layer on the baking sheet. Roast in the oven, turning once, until light golden brown, about 12 minutes. Remove from the oven and let cool before slicing into thin strips.

4. Pour the syrup into a small saucepan and bring to a simmer over low heat. Stir in the apricots, cinnamon, and pecans. Serve warm.

BANANAS FOSTER CRÊPES
WALNUTS, CRÈME FRAÎCHE

Bananas Foster was created in 1951 by Paul Blangé at Brennan's Restaurant in New Orleans, Louisiana. It was named for Richard Foster, a friend of Owen Brennan's who was then the city's Crime Commission chairman. If you have been fortunate enough to visit New Orleans and eat at Brennan's, then you know what an incredible dessert Bananas Foster is. Sautéed in a buttery, cinnamony caramel sauce and flambéed with dark rum and banana liqueur, bananas are then poured over creamy, rich vanilla ice cream. On the brunch menu at Bar Americain, I take all those yummy components, replacing the ice cream with a slightly tangy crème fraîche whipped cream, and pair them with delicate crêpes. These crêpes are served as an entrée and not a dessert. I can't think of a better way to start off my weekend.

Serves 4

Crêpes

¾ cup all-purpose flour
2 tablespoons granulated sugar
⅛ teaspoon fine salt
¾ cup whole milk
3 large eggs
3 tablespoons unsalted butter, melted and cooled, plus more for the pan

Fillings and Toppings

¾ cup heavy cream, very cold
3 tablespoons crème fraîche
Pinch of ground cinnamon
2 ripe bananas, peeled and sliced ¼ inch thick
1 cup walnuts, toasted (see page 250) and coarsely chopped
Caramel Sauce (recipe follows), warm
2 tablespoons confectioners' sugar mixed with ½ teaspoon ground cinnamon
Fresh mint sprigs (optional), for garnish

1. To make the crêpes, whisk together the flour, granulated sugar, and salt in a medium bowl. Whisk together the milk, 2 tablespoons water, the eggs, and the butter in a small bowl. Add to the flour mixture and whisk to combine. Cover and let sit at room temperature for 30 minutes or refrigerate for up to 1 day.

2. Line a large plate with parchment or wax paper. Heat a crêpe pan or an 8-inch nonstick skillet over medium heat and brush the bottom and sides with melted butter. Add 3 tablespoons crêpe batter to the skillet and immediately tilt and swirl the skillet to spread the batter evenly over the bottom. Cook until the center of the crêpe is cooked through and the edges are lightly browned, about 1 minute. Gently flip and cook the other side for 20 seconds. Invert the crêpe onto the prepared plate. Repeat with the remaining batter, placing parchment paper between crêpes. The crêpes can be made 1 day in advance, covered, and refrigerated.

3. To make the topping, whip the heavy cream with a handheld electric mixer or a balloon whisk until soft peaks form, add the crème fraîche and cinnamon, and whisk until combined.

4. Place the crêpes, pale side up, on a flat surface, arrange 5 slices of banana down the center of each crêpe, and roll tightly. Place 2 crêpes on each of 4 large plates and add a few slices of banana. Top with a large dollop of the whipped cream and chopped walnuts and spoon some of the caramel sauce over the crêpes. Dust with some of the cinnamon confectioners' sugar and garnish with mint sprigs if desired.

CARAMEL SAUCE
Makes about 1 cup

   1 cup sugar
   1 cup heavy cream
   ¼ teaspoon ground cinnamon
   1 tablespoon orange liqueur,
      such as Grand Marnier
   1 tablespoon dark rum

1. Combine the sugar and ½ cup water in a medium saucepan and bring to a boil over high heat, swirling the pot occasionally (do not stir) to even out the color. Cook until deep amber in color, about 8 minutes.

2. While the caramel is cooking, pour the heavy cream into a small saucepan and bring to a simmer over low heat. Remove from the heat and keep warm.

3. When the caramel has reached a deep amber color, slowly whisk in the heavy cream. Be careful, the hot mixture will bubble. Whisk until smooth. Remove from the heat and stir in the cinnamon, orange liqueur, and rum. The sauce can be cooled, covered, and refrigerated for up to 1 week. Reheat over low heat or in the microwave. Serve warm.

SAUCES AND STOCKS

BAR AMERICAIN BARBECUE SAUCE

This southwest-inspired house barbecue sauce is used on its own or as the base of many sauces at Bar Americain. It is slightly sweet from the molasses, honey, and brown sugar and slightly earthy from the dried red chiles. It is the perfect sauce slathered on smoked ribs (page 149), or spiced up and spooned onto grilled oysters on the half shell (page 72). Adding bourbon transports this sauce from Sante Fe to Kentucky in a matter of minutes.

Makes about 2½ cups

2 tablespoons canola oil

1 large Spanish onion, coarsely chopped

5 cloves garlic, coarsely chopped

½ cup red wine vinegar

2 (16-ounce) cans plum tomatoes, pureed with their juices

5 dried red New Mexico chiles, stemmed, seeded, and coarsely chopped

1 cup ketchup

¼ cup Worcestershire sauce

3 tablespoons Dijon mustard

3 tablespoons dark brown sugar

2 tablespoons honey

¼ cup molasses

1 tablespoon pure maple syrup

Kosher salt and freshly ground black pepper

1. Heat the oil in a heavy medium saucepan over medium-high heat. Add the onion and cook until soft, about 4 minutes. Add the garlic and cook for 1 minute. Stir in the vinegar and cook until reduced by half, 2 minutes. Add the pureed tomatoes, 1 cup water, and the chiles, bring to a boil, and simmer for 10 minutes.

2. Add the ketchup, Worcestershire, mustard, brown sugar, honey, and molasses and simmer, stirring occasionally, until thickened, 30 to 40 minutes.

3. Transfer the mixture to a food processor and puree until smooth. Return the mixture to a medium saucepan over high heat, add the maple syrup, and cook until slightly thickened, about 5 minutes. Season with salt and pepper. Pour into a bowl and allow to cool. The sauce will keep, stored in a tightly sealed container, in the refrigerator for 1 week.

VARIATION
BOURBON BARBECUE SAUCE
Makes about 3 cups

Bring 2 cups bourbon to a boil in a small saucepan over high heat and cook until reduced by half to 1 cup, about 4 minutes. Whisk in ½ cup lightly packed dark brown sugar and cook, whisking occasionally, until thickened and the sugar melts, about 4 minutes. Remove from the heat and let sit at room temperature. Add to Bar Americain Barbecue Sauce when you add the maple syrup.

HABANERO-MANGO HOT SAUCE

I sometimes use this full-flavored hot sauce to spice up my Crab-Coconut Cocktail (page 79). It is also wonderful drizzled over raw oysters and clams and is one of the sauces served with the raw bar selections at Bar Americain. You must use really ripe mangoes for the best possible flavor. Also, it is extremely important to be very careful when handling the habanero. We use plastic gloves when working with these super-hot chiles, but whatever you do, make sure to keep your hands away from your face (especially your eyes!) until they are absolutely clean.

Makes 2 cups

2 tablespoons canola oil

1 small red onion, coarsely chopped

2 cloves garlic, chopped

3 ripe mangoes, peeled, pitted, and diced

1 habanero chile, halved and seeded

1 cup rice wine vinegar

Kosher salt

1 to 2 tablespoons honey, depending on the sweetness of the mangoes

1. Heat the oil in a medium saucepan over high heat. Add the onion and cook until soft, about 4 minutes. Add the garlic and cook for 30 seconds. Add the mangoes, habanero, and ½ cup water and cook, stirring occasionally, until the mangoes are very soft, about 5 minutes.

2. Add the vinegar and cook over low heat for 2 minutes. Carefully transfer the mixture to a blender and blend until smooth. Season with salt and honey to taste. If the mixture is too thick, add a few table- spoons water. Strain the mixture through a strainer set over a small bowl. Let cool to room temperature. The sauce can be made 1 week in advance and stored covered in the refrigerator.

GREEN CHILE SAUCE

This sauce is wonderful served on its own, but paired with Red Chile Sauce (opposite) and served with eggs (Blue Corn Fried Eggs, page 219) or fish or pork or chicken, it becomes known as Christmas. Why? Christmas is known for its red and green colors! In New Mexico restaurant lingo (Sante Fe to be exact), *Christmas* means a plate of half-red and half-green chile sauces. The New Mexico terminology has spread to some other states in the Southwest, such as Arizona and Texas.

Makes about 1¼ cups

7 tomatillos, husked and rinsed

2 poblano chiles, coarsely chopped

2 jalapeño chiles, chopped

1 small red onion, chopped

3 cloves garlic

3 tablespoons canola oil

Kosher salt and freshly ground black pepper

½ cup chopped fresh cilantro

1 tablespoon honey

1. Preheat the oven to 400°F.

2. Toss the tomatillos, poblanos, jalapeños, onion, and garlic in the oil on a baking sheet and season with salt and pepper. Roast, turning once, until the vegetables are golden brown and soft, 20 to 30 minutes. Let cool slightly.

3. Transfer to a food processor and process with the cilantro, adding a little water if necessary to adjust the consistency, until pureed. Season with the honey and additional salt and pepper if needed. The sauce can be made 1 day in advance and stored in a container with a tight-fitting lid in the refrigerator. Heat gently before serving.

RED CHILE SAUCE

The counterpart to Green Chile Sauce (opposite) and a darn good sauce on its own served with meat and fish. Brick red New Mexico chiles give this sauce great color and a deep roasted earthy flavor.

Makes about 1¼ cups

10 New Mexico chiles, stemmed, seeded, and chopped
7 garlic cloves, chopped
1 small Spanish onion, chopped
½ cup packed dark brown sugar
2 tablespoons honey
2 tablespoons red wine vinegar
Kosher salt and freshly ground black pepper

1. Combine the chiles, garlic, onion, brown sugar, and 1 quart water in a large saucepan and bring to a boil over high heat. Reduce the heat and simmer until the chiles are very soft, about 30 minutes.

2. Transfer the solids to a food processor using a slotted spoon and add 1 cup of the cooking liquid. Process until smooth, adding more of the cooking liquid to reach a thick but pourable sauce consistency. Season the sauce with the honey, vinegar, and salt and pepper to taste. The sauce can be refrigerated for up to 1 day. Reheat before serving.

CHIVE OIL

This emerald-hued oil—along with the Parsley Oil variation—is used to put the finishing touch on many plates that leave Bar Americain's kitchen. Though admittedly I love it mostly for esthetic purposes, it does add a hint of fresh, herbal flavor too. You can make either of these in advance and refrigerate for up to 2 days; bring to room temperature before serving.

Makes about ¾ cup

½ cup chopped fresh chives
¼ cup fresh spinach leaves
½ cup canola oil
½ teaspoon kosher salt

Combine the chives, spinach, canola oil, and salt in a blender and blend for 1 minute. Strain through a coarse strainer lined with cheesecloth into a bowl.

VARIATION
PARSLEY OIL

Replace the chives with 1½ cups packed fresh flat-leaf parsley leaves. Proceed as directed.

CHICKEN STOCK

This full-flavored stock is the base of many of our soups and sauces at Bar Americain. Make a double batch and freeze it in 1-quart containers so you always have some on hand. In a pinch, low-sodium canned chicken broth will work in soup recipes. However, because chicken broth is not made with chicken bones and therefore doesn't contain any gelatin, canned broth is not recommended for any of the chicken stock–based sauces in this book.

Makes about 2 quarts

5 pounds raw chicken carcasses, rinsed
    well and coarsely chopped
3 tablespoons canola oil
2 medium Spanish onions, quartered
    (do not peel)
2 large stalks celery, plus leaves, coarsely
    chopped
2 large carrots, coarsely chopped
8 sprigs fresh thyme
12 sprigs fresh flat-leaf parsley
1 bay leaf
1 teaspoon black peppercorns

1. Preheat the oven to 400°F.

2. Put the chicken carcasses in a large roasting pan and toss with the oil. Roast in the oven, turning once, until deep golden brown, 15 to 20 minutes.

3. Transfer the carcasses to a large stockpot and add 3½ quarts cold water, the onions, celery, carrots, thyme, parsley, bay leaf, and peppercorns. Bring to a boil over high heat, reduce the heat to medium-low, and simmer, skimming the surface occasionally, for 2 hours.

4. Strain the stock through a cheesecloth-lined strainer into a medium pot and discard the solids. Boil over high heat until reduced by half to about 2 quarts. Let cool to room temperature and then refrigerate until cold, at least 8 hours or overnight. Once cold, remove the top layer of fat that will have risen to the top and discard. Return to the refrigerator for up to 2 days or freeze for up to 3 months.

LOBSTER STOCK

Making homemade lobster stock is relatively easy. If you don't steam a lot of lobsters at home or have access to lobster shells in your area—or making seafood or fish stocks simply isn't your thing—you can buy good-quality prepared fish/seafood stocks from your local fishmonger or online (see Sources).

Makes about 2½ quarts

2 tablespoons canola oil
3 pounds lobster shells (from 4 2-pound
    lobsters), coarsely chopped
½ cup brandy
½ cup dry sherry
1 tablespoon tomato paste
2 plum tomatoes, chopped
1 medium Spanish onion, chopped
2 medium stalks celery, chopped
12 sprigs fresh flat-leaf parsley
6 sprigs fresh thyme
1 bay leaf
12 black peppercorns

1. Heat the oil in a large stockpot over high heat until it begins to smoke. Add the lobster shells and cook, stirring occasionally, for 5 minutes. Add the brandy and sherry and boil until completely evaporated. Stir in the tomato paste and cook for 30 seconds.

2. Add the tomatoes, onion, celery, parsley, thyme, bay leaf, peppercorns, and 3 quarts cold water. Bring to a boil over high heat, reduce the heat to medium-low, and simmer, skimming the surface occasionally, for 45 minutes.

3. Strain the stock though a strainer lined with cheesecloth into a large bowl, pressing on the solids to extract as much liquid as possible; discard the solids. Let the stock come to room temperature; then cover and refrigerate for up to 2 days or freeze for up to 3 months.

SHRIMP STOCK

Everyone loves shrimp, so the next time you make a batch of Gulf Shrimp and Grits (page 80) or Shrimp-Tomatillo Cocktail (page 75), save the shells and freeze them until you have enough for stock. However, you can also purchase prepared shrimp stock from your fishmonger or online (see Sources).

Makes about 2 quarts

    3 tablespoons canola oil
    5 cups (about 2 pounds) raw shrimp shells, heads, and tails, rinsed well
    1 medium yellow onion, coarsely chopped
    1 small carrot, coarsely chopped
    1 stalk celery, coarsely chopped
    1 cup dry white wine
    2 plum tomatoes, coarsely chopped
    10 sprigs fresh flat-leaf parsley
    1 bay leaf
    1/2 teaspoon black peppercorns

1. In a large saucepan over high heat, heat the oil until almost smoking. Add the shrimp shells, onion, carrot, and celery and sauté, stirring occasionally, for 5 minutes. Add the wine and boil until reduced by half. Add 2 1/2 quarts cold water, the tomatoes, parsley, bay leaf, and peppercorns. Bring to a boil, reduce the heat to medium-low, and simmer, skimming the surface occasionally, for 40 minutes.

2. Strain the stock though a strainer lined with cheesecloth into a large bowl, pressing on the solids to extract as much liquid as possible; discard the solids. Let the stock come to room temperature; then cover and refrigerate for up to 2 days or freeze for up to 3 months.

VEGETABLE STOCK

We use this stock for Pumpkin Soup (page 29) but you can use it for any vegetable-based soup of your liking. The addition of canela in the stock works well with the pumpkin and adds a slightly warm, spicy note to the base.

Makes about 1 1/2 quarts

    1 medium Spanish onion, quartered
    1 large carrot, coarsely chopped
    1 large stalk celery, coarsely chopped
    8 sprigs fresh flat-leaf parsley
    1 bay leaf
    1 Mexican cinnamon (canela) stick
    6 black peppercorns
    Kosher salt and freshly ground black pepper

1. Put the onion, carrot, celery, parsley, bay leaf, cinnamon stick, and peppercorns in a medium saucepan, add 2 quarts cold water, and bring to a boil over high heat. Reduce the heat to medium-low and simmer, skimming occasionally, for 45 minutes.

2. Strain the stock through a strainer lined with cheesecloth into a bowl, pressing on the vegetables to extract as much liquid as possible; discard the solids. Season lightly with salt and pepper. Let the stock come to room temperature; then cover and refrigerate for up to 2 days or freeze for up to 3 months.

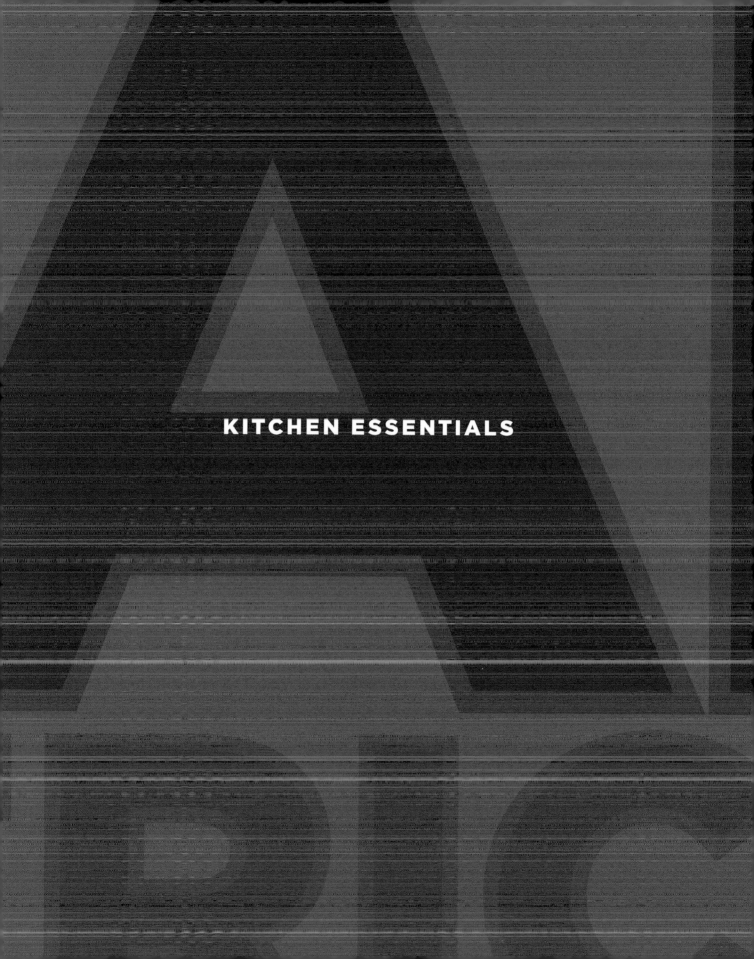

KITCHEN ESSENTIALS

THE AMERICAN PANTRY

I call a well-stocked pantry a culinary arsenal, because it allows you to prepare a multitude of recipes on short notice. People always ask me what I keep on hand at home and in the restaurants, so here are lists of my basics. For the most part, if you have these ingredients around, all you will probably need to pick up at the grocery store is a protein and some produce. Remember that your refrigerator should be viewed as a pantry too, where items that last longer than a few days, such as dairy products, condiments, and of course bacon, should always be stocked.

BAKING

All-purpose flour, unbleached

Baking powder

Baking soda

Chocolate, milk, semisweet, and bittersweet

Cocoa powder, unsweetened Dutch processed

Nonstick cooking spray

Salt, fine sea

Sugar, confectioners', granulated, and light and dark brown

Vanilla beans

Vanilla extract, pure

CANNED GOODS

Beans

Bell peppers, roasted red

Chipotle chiles in adobo sauce

Coconut milk, unsweetened

Plum tomatoes, whole

Stocks, low-sodium chicken and vegetable

CONDIMENTS

Anchovies, packed in oil

Capers, small, packed in brine

Honey, clover

Horseradish, grated

Ketchup

Maple syrup, grade B pure

Mayonnaise

Molasses, regular (not blackstrap) and pomegranate (see Sources)

Mustard, Dijon and whole grain

Pickles, dill and cornichons

Worcestershire sauce

DRIED HERBS AND SPICES

Allspice, ground

Bay leaves

Cinnamon, whole sticks and ground

Cloves, whole

Cayenne pepper

Chile powders, pure (various)

Coriander, whole seed and ground

Cumin, whole seed and ground

Nutmeg, whole

Paprika, smoked sweet Spanish

Peppercorns, whole black and white

Salt, kosher

Tabasco or other hot sauce

Tomato powder (see Sources)

OILS AND VINEGARS

Canola oil

Extra virgin olive oil

White truffle oil (optional)

Apple cider vinegar

Balsamic vinegar

Red wine vinegar

Rice vinegar

White wine vinegar

FRESH PRODUCE

Carrots

Celery

Chiles, fresh (various)

Citrus (oranges, lemons, limes)

Garlic

Herbs (various)

Shallots

Onions, red, sweet, and Spanish

Potatoes, Idaho (Russet) and sweet

REFRIGERATOR STAPLES

Bacon, double-smoked

Butter, unsalted

Cream, heavy

Crème fraîche or sour cream

Eggs, large

Milk, whole

Nuts (various)

FREEZER STAPLES

Frozen fruits (various)

Frozen vegetables (corn and peas)

EQUIPMENT ESSENTIALS

On my website, bobbyflay.com, I have a section called "Ask Bobby" where people can write in and ask questions about cooking, my restaurants, shows, etc. One of the most frequently asked questions revolves around what equipment you need to cook at home.

The truth is you don't need much—but quality counts. In fact, I think one of the most important things you can do, if you are serious about cooking, is to invest in solid, well-made tools and vessels. Learning how to cook with minimal equipment will teach you how to be a more efficient cook, will save you money, and, if you live in a city like New York, will save you space.

The following are items that I feel all home kitchens should have. I've also included a few wish list items that serious cooks might want to consider. Stainless steel is a must for utensils, pots, and pans, unless otherwise noted.

UTENSILS AND EQUIPMENT

Measuring spoons

Dry measuring cups

Glass liquid measuring cup

Box grater

Microplane grater

Vegetable peeler

Peppermill

Wide stainless-steel spatula

Rubber spatulas, preferably heat resistant

Wooden spoons

Slotted spoons

Ladles

Tongs

Wire skimmer or "spider"

Wire whisks

Instant-read thermometer, for meat

Candy/deep-fat thermometer, for cooking sugar and for frying

Baster (optional)

Biscuit cutter (optional)

Mandoline (optional)

Stainless-steel mixing bowls

Colander

Strainers: fine-mesh and coarse-mesh

Cutting boards: wood for vegetables, bread, and fruit; plastic for onions, garlic, fish, meat, and poultry

KNIVES

Chef's knife, 10-inch

Paring knife

Serrated knife

Steak knives

Sharpening steel

Carving knife (optional)

Boning knife (optional)

BAKING EQUIPMENT

Glass or ceramic baking dishes

Round cake pans

Rimmed baking sheets

Glass pie plates

Loaf pans

Muffin tins

Wire cooling racks

Wood rolling pin

Pastry brushes

Parchment paper or silicone baking mats

POTS AND PANS

Broiler pan

Cast-iron skillet

Cast-iron grill or griddle pan

Enamel-coated cast-iron Dutch oven, 7- or 9-quart

Frying pans or shallow sauté pans, 10- and 12-inch

Deep sauté pan with lid, 4- or 6-quart

Saucepans, 2- and 3-quart

Stockpot, 8- or 12-quart

Roasting pan with rack, at least 14 x 11-inch

APPLIANCES

Coffee grinders: one for coffee and one to grind whole spices (optional)

Blender

Food processor

Stand mixer

Toaster

Waffle iron (optional)

Kitchen scale (optional)

Hand mixer (optional)

Immersion blender (optional)

COOKING TECHNIQUES

I cover the gamut in this book when it comes to the various cooking techniques used at Bar Americain. Following is a glossary of terms and techniques you will find helpful when cooking from this book.

BLANCHING (OR PARBOILING)

This term means to plunge foods into boiling salted water for a few seconds or a few minutes, depending on what you are cooking. It is used for fruits to make the skin easy to peel or to set the color of green vegetables without really cooking them. The food does not cook all the way through and is typically cooked again with another technique, so crisp texture is what you are looking for. Once blanched, the ingredients should be scooped out and placed in ice water to stop the cooking and set the color of the vegetables.

BRAISING

Used for tougher cuts of meat to make them more tender, braising involves searing meat in hot fat to enhance its flavor and then cooking it in liquid (I prefer stock) in a low oven so that it cooks slowly and gently. Adding wine or another acid such as vinegar or tomatoes to the braising liquid will further tenderize the meat. Braising relies on heat, time, and moisture to break down tough connective tissue and collagens in meat, making it an ideal way to cook tougher cuts.

BROILING

In the United States, broiling refers to a method of cooking where the heat is applied from above. In electric ovens, this is accomplished with a heating element. Sometimes the food is placed near the upper heating element to intensify the heat. The lower heating element may or may not be left off, and the oven door is sometimes opened partially. Gas ovens often have a separate compartment for broiling, sometimes a drawer below the bottom flame. Broiling is also used for toasting, as well as browning the tops of gratin dishes, melting cheeses onto sandwiches, and caramelizing a sugar crust.

COLD-SMOKING

Cold-smoking imparts a subtle smoky flavor to meat, fish, and vegetables. Since no actual cooking takes place during this process, further preparation, such as roasting, grilling, or sautéing, is required.

To cold-smoke: Prepare a small charcoal or wood fire in a domed grill or in a stovetop cold-smoker. Lay chips of soaked aromatic wood, such as hickory, apple, or mesquite, over the ashes—you just want to get some smoke going, not a very hot fire. (Remember that you aren't cooking the food, just infusing it with a smoky flavor.) Arrange the food on the grill rack over the chips, open the top vent slightly, and cover the grill so that the smoke stays inside. Smoke tomatoes (rub with oil first) for 10 minutes; steaks, chicken pieces, or duck breasts for 15 minutes; whole chickens for 20 minutes.

GRILLING

Most people familiar with my cooking know that I love to grill and have written several cookbooks dedicated to the subject alone. Grilling is a form of cooking that involves dry radiant heat from below and takes place on a charcoal or gas grill. My preferred grill is a gas grill because it is fast and clean. I also am a huge advocate of cast-iron grill pans that can be used on top of the stove.

PANFRYING

Not to be confused with sautéing (see page 250), this is a form of frying characterized by the use of less cooking oil (I prefer to use canola) than deep-frying, using enough oil to, at most, cover the food to be cooked only halfway. Panfrying usually requires the use of a frying pan, which is deeper than a sauté pan. I like to use cast iron, but a good heavy stainless steel pan will work well also. Because of the partial coverage, the food must be flipped at least once to cook both sides.

PAN ROASTING

I use this technique, not to be confused with roasting (below), a lot at my restaurants for smaller, thicker cuts of meat or fish. This method consists of searing on top of the stove and quickly finishing the cooking in a very hot oven. You get a great dark crust and even cooking.

REDUCING TO A SAUCE CONSISTENCY

Chefs use this term a lot, and it simply means to boil the liquid until it thickens. I use this method to thicken my sauces naturally, without the help of a gummy thickening agent such as flour or corn-starch. The best way to test for sauce consistency is to dip a spoon into the sauce—the sauce should cling to the spoon. Next, run your finger through the sauce on the spoon; if the line your finger made stays and the sauce doesn't run back into it, you are good to go. Reaching sauce consistency requires using homemade stock or a good-quality canned or boxed stock for your sauces. Store-bought *broths,* while convenient, are not always made with bones and therefore have no natural gelatin in them. As a result, they will not thicken sauces and will not give you the richest possible flavor.

ROASTING

Roasting is a dry-heat method of cooking in a very hot oven using an uncovered pan (roasting pan) to avoid steaming. Hot air circulates around the food, ensuring that it cooks evenly on all sides. This method of cooking is best for large cuts of meat and fish and creates a beautiful caramelization on the exterior of the meat, which adds incredible flavor.

To roast garlic: Preheat the oven to 325°F. Separate the cloves of a head of garlic, but do not peel. Drizzle the cloves with canola oil and season with salt and pepper. Wrap the garlic securely in aluminum foil and place on a baking sheet. Roast in the oven for 45 minutes to 1 hour. Pop the cloves out of the skins before using. Covered tightly, roasted garlic will keep in the refrigerator for up to 2 days

To roast peppers and chiles: Preheat the oven to 400°F. Brush the peppers with canola oil and season with salt and pepper. Place in the oven on a rimmed baking sheet and rotate until charred on all sides, about 35 minutes. Remove from the oven. Transfer the peppers to a bowl, cover with plastic wrap, and let sit for 15 minutes to allow the skin to loosen. Then peel, halve, and seed. Treat chiles exactly the same way as the peppers. Roasted peppers and chiles can be covered and stored for up to 5 days in the refrigerator.

SAUTÉING

Sautéing means cooking food quickly in a shallow pan with a small amount of fat over fairly high heat. Ingredients are usually cut into pieces or thinly sliced to facilitate fast cooking. Food that is sautéed is browned while preserving its texture, moisture, and flavor. Fats with high burning points, such as pure olive oil, vegetable or canola oil, and clarified butter, are commonly used for sautéing.

TOASTING

Toasting brings out the flavor of nuts, seeds, and spices. It can be done in the oven or on the stovetop; I prefer the even heat of an oven, which is less likely to burn the nuts in spots.

To toast nuts or seeds: Preheat the oven to 350°F. Put a single layer of nuts in a skillet or on a baking sheet and toast, shaking the pan every couple of minutes to prevent burning, until lightly golden brown and fragrant, 5 to 7 minutes.

To toast spices, proceed as for nuts, but toast until just fragrant, only 3 to 4 minutes.

To toast coconut, proceed as for nuts, but toast for 8 to 10 minutes, stirring occasionally.

SOURCES

Bobby Flay Spice Rubs and Sauces
bobbyflay.com

Cheeses
murrayscheese.com

Double-Smoked Bacon, Ham
www.newsomscountryham.com

Duck, Game
dartagnan.com

Fish, Shrimp, Meat, Chicken, and Veal Stocks
clubsauce.com

Fresh Seafood
shop.legalseafood.com

Pistachio Paste
kingarthurflour.com

Pomegranate Molasses, Spices, Vanilla Beans, Vanilla Extract
kalustyans.com

Tomato Powder, Vanilla Beans, Vanilla Extract
thespicehouse.com
847-328-3711

Cast-Iron Pans, Grill Pans
Bobby Flay line at
kohls.com

Kitchen Gadgets/Utensils
cuisipro.com
kitchenaid.com

Knives
kershawknives.com

Pots and Pans
allclad.com
mauviel.com

INDEX

AMERICANS AT WAR

Society, Culture, and the Homefront

VOLUME 1: 1500–1815

John P. Resch, Editor in Chief

MACMILLAN REFERENCE USA
An imprint of Thomson Gale, a part of The Thomson Corporation

Detroit • New York • San Francisco • San Diego • New Haven, Conn. • Waterville, Maine • London • Munich

Americans at War: Culture, Society, and the Homefront

John P. Resch, Editor in Chief

LIBRARY OF CONGRESS CATALOGING-IN-PUBLICATION DATA

Americans at war : society, culture, and the homefront/John P. Resch, Editor in Chief.
   p. cm.
     Includes bibliographical references and index.
     ISBN 0-02-865806-X (set hardcover : alk. paper)—ISBN 0-02-865807-8 (v. 1)—
     ISBN 0-02-865808-6 (v. 2)—ISBN 0-02-865809-4 (v. 3)—ISBN 0-02-865810-8
     (v. 4)—ISBN 0-02-865993-7 (e-book)
     1. United States—History, Military. 2. United States—Social conditions.
     3. United States—Social life and customs. 4. War and society—United
     States—History. I. Resch, John Phillips

E181.A453 2005
973—dc22   2004017314

This title is also available as an e-book.
ISBN 0-02-865993-7
Contact your Thomson Gale sales representative for ordering information.

Printed in the United States of America
10 9 8 7 6 5 4 3 2 1